THREE MEN IN A VAN

GUILDFORD TO GIBRALTAR
BY THE BACK ROADS

JEREMY HASTINGS

1

What with one thing and another the three of us hadn't met up for over three months, so when I walked into the Eagle's Head Inn at Over Kellet, near Carnforth, I was pleased to see Harry and Geoff sitting at our usual table with their pints of bitter. Geoff, already talking nineteen to the dozen, sprang up and shot to the bar to get my pint, so I was able to greet Harry in our usual manner.

"All right?"

"Yep. You?"

"Fine. What's the Boy Wonder been going on about?" I asked, as at a mere fifty-three Geoff was the younger component of the trio by five or six years. Harry and I go way back – we met in the Cub Scouts – while Geoff latched onto us at our local pub in Lancaster about fifteen years ago and, despite our less frequent meetings of late, we still haven't been able to shake him off.

"Oh, this and that. Did you know he'd come into some money?"

"I believe so. Was it an aunt who died?"

"Yes, so he's packed in his job at the hotel," Harry said through frothy lips.

"I guess she left him a lot then."

"Not enough, I bet, but we know Geoff and work have never seen eye to eye."

While Harry had just had the one job – as a police officer, recently retired – Geoff had a CV as long as his arm and maybe half a leg. I'd been a history teacher in Lancaster until the year before, when my wife and I had retired and moved up to Carnforth. Harry was still living in Lancaster – in a flat for the time being until he and his soon-to-be ex-wife sold their house – while Geoff had scarpered to Kendal about four years after we'd met, due to yet another of his 'clinging women', none of whom had been able to entice him to the altar or registry office.

"Jeremy, you old git! How's things?" was Geoff's loud greeting as he loped across the busy pub and plonked down my pint.

"Fine. So you're a rich man, Geoff," I said after submitting my hand to the usual firm squeeze from his bony fingers. Geoff is five feet nine and ten stone of pure sinewy energy, and if he had only found his true calling – as he often declared – he'd have been a world-beater. I won't list his career history, as he's sure to mention many of his previous jobs during the course of this narrative.

"Not *rich*, as such, but being a man of ascetic nature I've got plenty for the time being."

"Asc-*what*-ic nature?" Harry asked with furrowed brow, he being the less cultured of the three.

"Austere, almost monkish."

"Monkfish?" Harry enquired, as he also had by far the worst auditory powers, but was still in denial about his need for a hearing aid and already an adept lip reader. Geoff once bought him a rusty ear trumpet at a car boot sale, which brought on one of his infrequent but scary bursts of wrath, Harry being a large man – about six feet one and of undisclosed weight. (I'm somewhere between the two of them in height, weight and temperament.)

"Monk*ish*, as in like a monk, at least where money is concerned. Frugal, thrifty, prudent."

"All right, smart arse," said Harry, before downing a third of his pint. "Shame we can only have one and a half," he added, as being an ex-copper he was a stickler for the law, on our shores at least, as you'll see in due course.

"I feel like I deserve a break from work anyway. It was all right for you two, as you found your vocations early on, but I'm still searching. I shall have a year off, I think, but I must do something with my time. Any ideas?"

"You could write a book," I suggested.

"Or become a real monk, in Tibet... or further away," said Harry with a grin.

"Hmm, travel is one option that I've been mulling over. I've been thinking that now you two are retired we might head off somewhere together," he said, beaming at each of us in turn.

Harry fidgeted and I pointed to my wedding ring, so Geoff put down his glass and eyeballed Harry. Geoff has penetrating blue eyes and Harry's placid brown ones began to idly scan the room.

"What?" he finally said when there was nothing left to look at.

"Harry, you've retired and you're also finally free of the bonds of matrimony. What say we head off around the world and send Jeremy postcards from far-flung places?"

"Around the world? Me and you? No, no, I don't think so, somehow." His cheeks wobbled as he shook his head. He'd put on weight since retiring and though it was still fairly evenly distributed – his pot belly wasn't huge – it was about time he began to move those massive limbs of his. The idea of the two of them heading off together, however, was preposterous. I doubted they'd reach the airport without falling out, as although they're fond of each other, in a way, they're too different to get along alone together. Harry is a down-to-earth, no-nonsense type of bloke, while Geoff is the archetypal dreamer – a cross between Don Quixote and Walter Mitty, with a bit of Don Juan thrown in for good measure, as he's not bad looking for a skinny chap. I've always been the middleman who has helped them to see each other's good qualities and without me they wouldn't get far.

Still, Geoff was set on taking a trip, Harry needed a change of air, and I wasn't averse to a boys' holiday myself. Me and June – my wife of thirty-one years – love each other dearly, but now that we'd both retired from teaching and our daughter Chloe had long flown the nest there was nothing to stop me shooting off for... how long? A fortnight would surely be a cinch to secure and I thought that would be long enough for our first real holiday together, if you don't count the stag do to Amsterdam we went on ten years earlier, along with several more men set on upholding the tradition of disgracing our race on a three-day drinking binge. No, it would have to be a healthy, uplifting kind of jaunt that would bring out the best in us and enrich our lives.

"I believe I can hear the gears of your brain grinding," said Geoff, who had preferred to wait for my contribution before expounding his own travel ideas.

"Have you read Three Men in a Boat?" I asked them, to get the ball rolling.

"A long time ago, but I remember it well," said Geoff, a dreamy gleam appearing in his eyes.

"I think I saw a film of it once, with Michael Palin and... two more fellas," said Harry, to my relief, as had he not, Geoff would no doubt have provided a pedantic résumé that might well have put him off. I wasn't really thinking of a boating trip, but the essence of the book – three pals taking a holiday to shake off the dust of the city – was to be the starting point for our discussion.

"Yes, yes, a boat trip!" Geoff cried, slapping the table.

"I didn't mean..."

"But not a piddling row up the Thames. We could... we could... buy a little yacht and cruise the Med," Geoff enthused.

"Crazily expensive," I replied.

"Just crazy," said Harry. "I prefer dry land anyway."

"I only mentioned the book because it was about three men doing something a bit out of the ordinary," I said with hands raised, hoping to secure their attention for a couple of minutes. "Also because the three of them didn't see eye to eye about everything. Like us they were fine sat over a beer, but when they were thrown together day and night for a week or so their different characters... manifested themselves," I said, always loath to use unnecessarily long words in Harry's presence. "The book's hilarious, but I'm sure that on the actual trip there was quite a bit of friction, so we have to think carefully about where we go and how we travel."

"So you're up for it?" Geoff asked, baring his fine teeth in delight.

"I think June will let me go for a fortnight."

"Oh, that's not long enough," he said, folding his arms tightly and wrinkling up his narrow nose.

"Sounds plenty to me. I've never been anywhere for above a fortnight and it was always more than enough," said Harry. He and his ex, Debbie, had waited for the younger of their two children to become independent before separating and he once said that they'd both agreed that they should have married younger so that they could have divorced earlier, which I thought a curious way of looking at things, due, I deduced, to their love of their kids who wouldn't have existed had they not tied the knot. Harry said it was a happy divorce, all things considered, and that they felt like old friends when they occasionally met up.

"Well, never mind that for now," I said. "First let's decide what to do, then I'll worry about getting permission. If a boat trip is out, what other form of locomotion could we consider?"

"A plane," said Harry, "to somewhere nice and warm."

"I'm not going to a bloody tourist resort," said Geoff, shaking his finger. "I'd like to get away from our fellow countrymen for a while."

"A flight could take us anywhere," I countered, looking at Harry's empty glass. "The question is, what are we going to *do*?"

"Travel," said Harry.

"But how? What about a walking trip?"

"Oh, I'd not keep up with you two."

"You could do with the exercise," said Geoff, gently.

"I know, and I don't mind a bit of walking, but not all day long."

"How about camping?" I asked, before standing and heading to the bar for our halves. Camping struck me as a good plan and I wanted them to ponder the idea. When I returned Geoff was talking tents.

"…and another option would be a yurt, though it might be a bit tricky to carry."

"I'd want a tent that I could sit in a chair in when it's pissing down," said Harry. "Though I wouldn't fancy carrying the chair around everywhere."

"June and me have one we could take. It's a six man, so big enough for three, but quite lightweight, so we could easily carry it between us," I said, glad that progress was being made. "Where are we going to go anyway?"

"Somewhere warm," said Harry.

"France?" I asked, observing Geoff's pensive face and realising what he was thinking. "Or how about Spain?"

"Ah, Spain! España! How I miss that country! I spent the best years of my life there," he said, not for the first time.

"Two years, thirty years ago," said Harry.

"Just twenty-four years this September I was forced to return," he said wistfully. "Oh, Carmela! The best, most beautiful woman I ever met... but so–"

"Clinging!" Harry and I cried in unison, before clinking glasses. We'd often heard the story of his passionate affair with a young lady from Jaén, where he was teaching English, and how pressure from her clannish family had forced him to choose between wedding bells and flight. He'd chosen flight – one to Manchester – but often regretted his decision, especially over his cups during our more boozy get-togethers back in Lancaster. He hadn't set foot on Spanish soil since then – due to other commitments or lack of funds – but still considered himself a competent linguist and cultural ambassador.

"How about Spain then? If we go next month it shouldn't be too hot," I said, it then being the middle of April.

"Cycle camping!" Geoff cried, after one of his frequent bouts of lateral thinking. "The bike'll take the weight off your legs, Harry, and carry the luggage."

"Er..." Harry began, looking glum.

"Bikes have about thirty gears these days. It's just as easy to go uphill as downhill."

"Not quite," I said. Geoff was the only one of us who'd done any cycling to speak of in the last forty years. I'm quite fit through hiking a lot, but I'd struggle on a bike, and I just couldn't imagine Harry astride one. "Camping sounds good, but we either stay in one place or move about on public transport, and walk a bit."

Geoff ran his hand slowly through his full head of closely-cropped greying hair, a sign that the brain beneath had gone into overdrive. Harry has half a head of similar hair, while I alone buck the modern trend and still sport my wavy locks, now grey and starting ever nearer the top of my head, producing what I like to think of as a high, erudite forehead. It was Harry, however, who never appears to be thinking, who uttered the fateful words.

"How about a camper van?"

We all looked at each other with raised brows, but when I clasped my hands I felt my wedding ring.

"A nice idea, but far too expensive," I said, patting Geoff's arm in an attempt to temper his impending surge of enthusiasm. "I think even a second-hand one costs about twenty grand."

"Oh, I'm sure you can get one for *much* less than that," he said. "It only has to last one trip, after all. On the other hand, I could really get some use out of one now that I'm not working. I know! I'll buy one out of my aunt's money. How about that?"

"Just how much has your aunt left you?" I asked, feeling a need to know in order to counsel my friend sagely.

"£28,056.14, minus these," he said, lifting an expensive-looking brown suede shoe onto Harry's lap.

"Get off, you pillock." Harry swatted the foot off with his huge hand. "So, you buy a decent camper van with that, then you have to go back to work because you'll have nowt left. Very clever, I must say."

"Hmm, I hadn't thought of that," said the man who had sent me an effusive email when he'd packed in his four-nights-a-week hotel job two weeks previously. In my reply I'd approved of a sabbatical, as it sounded like a rotten job, especially on weekend nights, but warned him that the nearer he got to sixty, the harder it would be to get another job. I was aware that he knew that better than me, as his previous job had been as an employment adviser, and he'd promised to do nothing rash.

"So a camper van's out, I'm afraid," I said.

Geoff, however, is not so easily diverted. "I know! We could buy a cheap one between the three of us, then sell it when we get back."

"Oh, I don't think–" Harry began.

"I'm pretty handy, as you know, so if I tart it up I dare say we'll make a profit on it, or maybe I'll buy you boys out and take off somewhere else." The gleam in his eyes promised to be inextinguishable, so I nodded slowly while I thought. Neither Harry nor I were short of money and I didn't like to dismiss the idea out of hand. I looked at Harry, who was examining the bottom of his empty glass. When he licked his rather blubbery lips I knew a pronouncement was coming.

"I'd risk a grand or so, but I'd like to get most of it back, eventually," he said, to my surprise and Geoff's delight. "I like the idea of a camper van trip because wherever we stop we can all do as we like. You two can go off climbing hills while I potter around a bit."

"I doubt we'll get a camper for three thousand," I said.

"I know, but we'd get a normal van. We could take that tent of yours and maybe use the van if it chucks it down, though I doubt it'll rain in Spain," he said, which I thought an astute plan, given our resources. I too could spare a thousand, but doubted that June would approve of a larger outlay.

"You two leave this with me," said Geoff, raising his hands like a prophet, before leaning to let them fall on our shoulders.

"Give over," said Harry, who isn't overly tactile, though in the early days of his police career he'd been known to get quite hands-on with uncooperative miscreants, especially while on duty in Morecambe on summer Saturday nights. He thought Tasers a bit cissy, though his son Paul, also a cop, had already been reprimanded for being too trigger-happy.

"So you'll look for an old van then?" I asked.

"I will look for a *camper* van, gentlemen. I will trawl EBay until I find one within our price range. I will go to collect it. I will give it all the TLC it requires and before you know it we'll be boarding the ferry for Santander." He clapped, people stared, so he gripped the table in order to avoid further acoustic effects.

"Santan-*where*?" Harry asked.

"Santander is a lovely city on the north coast of Spain which I omitted to visit during my years in that delightful land. I propose that we pop over on the ferry from Portsmouth and head south from there."

I visualised the geography and recalled Harry's aversion to boats. "Why not Dover to Calais, or even the Chunnel?"

"Because I doubt that your charming wife will allow you to go for more than a month, Jeremy, and we don't want to waste half of it in France."

"A month? I should be so lucky."

"A fortnight's not really long enough though, is it?" the recently liberated Harry chipped in.

With four expectant eyes upon me I whistled through my teeth, something I do when I'm nervous and which the kids soon picked up on during the early stages of my teaching career. I cleared my throat. "I'll see how she feels about three weeks first."

"No, no, Jeremy," said Geoff, his forefinger cutting the air like a metronome gone berserk. "Due to my extensive experience I *know* women like the back of my… hand. Tell June that our educational tour will last for five weeks. If you sulk hard enough she'll let you go for a month. That's how their minds work, believe me."

"Not June's. I'll try for a month though. Nothing ventured, nothing gained."

"Good man."

Harry's eyes narrowed. "How long does that ferry take?"

"Oh, not long," said Geoff with nonchalance. "It just shoots down into the Bay of Biscay and before you know it we'll be home and dry."

"Will we come back that way too? I doubt that ferry will be cheap," I said, having an idea of the true length of the crossing.

"Hmm, let me think." He turned to Harry. "Can we have another half, to aid thought?"

"Go on then, but get some peanuts to soak it up."

Geoff bounded over to the bar.

"What do you think?" I asked Harry.

"I'm up for it. I could do with a change of scene," he said with a shrug. Though never prone to showing emotion, I could see that he was keen on the idea.

"I'll try to get a month. I doubt he'll find a camper for that money though. Should we cough up a bit more; two grand each, say?"

"No, leave things as they are. He'll spend more anyway, you'll see."

Three halves appeared on the table. "I've got it," Geoff mumbled, the bag of peanuts still between his teeth.

"What?" asked Harry, still unable to lip-read ventriloquists.

The peanuts fell. "I've got it, our plan."

"Go on," Harry said.

"Guess."

We both groaned. Geoff was all too fond of guessing games and we were a bit fed up of them after fifteen years. He'd once made us guess what he'd studied at Lancaster University and it had taken us four evenings down the pub to come up with the correct answer, and then only after I'd got hold of an old prospectus. It turned out that he'd taken his degree in something he called 'BEANO', or Behaviour in Organisations, a course of study that gave him a lifelong aversion to organisations of all kinds, especially those that he ended up working for, such as the accountancy firm where he failed to make the grade during the two years following his graduation. We'd guessed the colour of his new car – fuchsia; the name of his Spanish girlfriend – which he pronounced earlier; his favourite food – homemade mackerel ravioli; and the number of strings on the guitar he played at the time – eleven, to name but a few. Now we had to guess his plan, which at least had some relevance, so we decided to humour him.

"We start at Santander and return through France," I said to get the ball rolling.

"Nope."

"We tour round and come back the same way," said Harry.

"Too obvious."

I pictured a map of Spain and looked at it through Geoff's eyes. "We drive down to meet up with your old flame in Jaén, you whisk her off her feet, give the van to her family as compensation, and the four of us fly back from Malaga."

"She'll be too old for me now, though no doubt still stunningly beautiful," he said with a wistful smile. "You're sort of on the right lines though."

"The van stays in Spain?"

"Hmm, *sort* of."

"We flog it to some dumb Brit in Benidorm and fly back from Alicante," said Harry.

"Now you're really getting warm." He drummed his fingers on the table and leered at us.

"Torremolinos… no… Gibraltar! We sell it in Gibraltar and fly back," I said, getting goose pimples on my arms, something that didn't happen with the fuchsia car, Carmela's name etc.

"*Co*rrect, Jeremy," he cried, grasping my arm.

"I was just going to say that," Harry muttered.

"What do you think?" Geoff asked us both.

"The route sounds fine, but will anyone want the van?" I asked. "I think they drive on the right in Gibraltar too, so it's not an attractive proposition."

"Hmm, no-one drives very far there, but I believe you're right," said Geoff. "*But*, that's not an issue. There are bound to be folk around who want to drive back here, so someone's sure to snap it up."

"Do you really think you'll find a camper van for three grand?" I asked, now sure that I wouldn't recover my thousand.

"Certain. I mean, it won't be a VW or anything like that, but you'd be surprised what you can find if you cast your net wide enough. You leave that to me. Before you know it we'll be speeding down the M6 like Jack Kerouac and company."

"Jack who?" asked Harry.

"Someone in a book, who we *won't* be emulating," I said quickly and clearly. "I've still got to get the green light from June, remember."

"Call us tonight," said Geoff.

"It'll be late by the time I get back and I might need more time. I'll call you both within forty-eight hours."

Geoff clapped. "I'll start looking for the van. You can pay me later."

"Don't buy the first pile of junk you see," said Harry.

"Yes, don't be too impetuous," I said, before looking up and tapping my right temple. "Oh, we've got a wedding to go to on about the tenth of May, so we can't set off before then," I lied, as Geoff was perfectly capable of rolling up in some rusty heap before the week was out, and it was already Wednesday.

"Now, now. You both know that I've got an excellent eye for a bargain," he said.

I pictured the tricycle – a proper one for grownups – that he'd bought some years earlier and resold, at a huge loss, after falling off it three times on his first outing. I also recalled the Savannah Monitor – a huge, repellent lizard – that he'd bought as a pet while living in a studio flat in Kendal. The beast soon needed more *lebensraum* and ended up being collected by the RSPCA.

Harry simply said, "Hilda," the name of the lizard.

"Trike," I added.

"*All* right, but I was young and foolish then," he said with a dismissive wave of the hand.

"You were forty-three when you bought Hilda," I said.

"The Beijing Olympics were on when you got the trike," said Harry. "When was that, Jeremy?"

"2008"

"Ye of little faith! But have no fear, I shall spend our money wisely and well. I must be off." He stood up abruptly. "I await your call with bated breath, Jeremy. Adiós, amigos."

A minute later we heard his old Harley Davidson – another bargain – burst into life and roar off up the road.

"Well," I said.

"Well, well," echoed Harry.

"Something to look forward to, I guess."

"Yep."

"I'll call you after he's called us. We haven't committed ourselves yet," I said.

"Oh, I think we have. He'll be humming that Queen song now."

"Don't Stop Me Now?"

"That's the one."

June, to my surprise, acquiesced to my request in a matter of minutes. Taken aback, I asked her if she was having an affair with the postman – a repellently good-looking young chap who had once complimented her on her still slim figure.

"I wish. Maybe when you've gone. No, I think it'll do you good to get away with the lads, but I want you back within thirty days. When… I mean if Geoff's van breaks down, you just dump it, or him, and get to an airport. When are you thinking of setting off?"

I told her about the fictitious wedding in May. "So not long after that, I guess. Are you sure you don't mind me going?" I asked, now a little miffed by her readiness to see the back of me.

"Of course not. Now that we're retired we need to change our mindset. We've reached the autumn of our lives and have to make the most of the years we've got left."

"Neither of us is sixty yet."

"Your dad starting going loopy before he was seventy."

"True, but he'd worked with mercury and stuff," I said, as he'd been a research scientist in the fifties and sixties.

"And we worked with kids, whose noxious effects on ageing are yet to be studied thoroughly. Besides, me and Dorothy want to go on a yoga retreat to Croatia, if you remember. We'll go for a week or so while you're away."

"Right, fair enough," I said, before remembering that I hadn't broken the news about the shared ownership of our vehicle. "They're not cheap, those retreats, are they?"

"Quite reasonable, actually. Why? What else do you want?"

I told her about the thousand we'd each agreed to contribute to our home on wheels. "But I'll get it back when we sell it in Gibraltar, or somewhere."

"Fat chance. Still, what you'll save on hotels will pay for it."

I multiplied thirty by thirty, because it's easy. "That's true, I hadn't thought of that. Is it OK then?"

"Yes, except you'll never get a camper for three thousand."

"Geoff says he'll find one, somewhere."

"Just make sure it's got good brakes. You're never too far from an airport in Spain these days."

I called Geoff the following morning and told him the good news.

"Good old June. You're so lucky to have a modern, unclingy wife, Jeremy."

"She's going to Croa–"

"Anyway, as we speak I'm surveying the entire second-hand camper van market of Great Britain, on EBay, AutoTrader and sundry other sites. I have every conceivable vehicle at my fingertips and with a couple of clicks a suitable conveyance can be ours in an instant."

"*Don't* be hasty and remember our budget, Geoff. We can't set off for a month anyway," I said, glad that I'd invented the wedding.

"Have no fear. It's true that our limited capital does rule out about ninety… five percent of the market, but among the less fashionable vans of a certain age I've already earmarked a couple."

"Like what?"

"A Mazda Bongo that looks like it might go for not much over three grand."

"What year?"

"1996."

"Mileage?"

"Undisclosed."

"Location?"

"Lewis."

"Lewes, in Sussex?"

"No, the Isle of Lewis."

"What?"

"Just off Scotland."

"I know where it is. Stornoway, I suppose," I said to prove it.

"No, a little place called Borve up in the north. It's on EBay and isn't getting many bids."

"I'm not bloody surprised. It'll cost an arm and a leg to go and fetch it back."

"I'm looking at a nice Ford Transit conversion too, near Wrexham."

"That sounds more like it. What do you mean by conversion?"

"It's got a big mattress in the back, and he'll throw in a portaloo for another fifty quid."

"So it's a van, which is what Harry said we'd have to settle for."

"Er, well, yes, I suppose it is really. It looks riddled with rust too, so maybe I'll let that one go."

"Yes, do. We could buy an old van in Lancaster or Kendal easily enough."

"No, no, it must be a camper. It *will* be a camper. I'll keep you posted."

"OK, I'll tell Harry that I've got the green light," I said, and after hanging up I called him and yelled my news down the phone.

"You don't need to shout. I'm not deaf."

"And Geoff's searching far and wide for a van."

"What? It's a bad line."

"Geoff – is – looking – for – a – van. Speak – soon."

"Righty-ho."

2

On the seventeenth of May Harry and I met at Lancaster train station at seven in the morning.

"Early start, eh?" I said after kissing June goodbye.

"Too right. You got everything?"

"Yes." I patted the green sixty litre rucksack which my resourceful wife had bought me, so I could walk and hitch to the nearest town when the van broke down. "Tons of clothes, a good sleeping bag, a bivvy bag, books, etcetera."

"Why do you need a bivvy bag?"

I relayed my wife's conviction that we'd end up stranded miles from nowhere. "But you'll be all right. You've got plenty of fat to keep you warm, in the worst case scenario."

"Hmm, I plan to lose at least a stone over the next month. It's a resolution, so I'll be doing plenty of walking."

I looked at his huge holdall. "That's good, because we've got to walk about two miles across London from Euston to Waterloo, though we could take the tube."

"Nope, we'll walk. I wish he'd found a van nearer than Guildford, or at least driven it up north like he'd promised to."

"Well, it's a mixed blessing, really. It's only forty-odd miles from there to Portsmouth. I've a feeling that the van's going to be an embarrassment, but I don't mind looking daft in Spain," I said as the train pulled in.

"I wish the bugger had told us what kind it is."

"I refused to guess."

"Me too. He sounds suited with it, so it might not be that bad after all."

"For £3,380? I'm prepared for the worst. It's got eight months MOT though, so the brakes ought to work."

Harry lugged his holdall onto the train with difficulty. He's as strong as an ox, so when he'd staggered to our seats I asked him what the hell he had in it.

"I look at it this way, Jeremy. Like June, I think the van might break down anytime, anywhere, so we must be prepared for every eventuality."

"So…?"

"What does man need? Food, clothing and shelter, nothing more. You've got your bivvy bag, I've got a two-man tent – one-man in my case – plus plenty of clothes, of course, and *tons* of food."

"Dehydrated?"

"No, we might be miles from water. Help me to lift it onto the rack."

We strained and the bag clunked.

"Tins?" I asked.

"Of every description. Beans, soups, rice pudding, curry, corned beef. You name it, it's in there. Seven days rations."

"For you?"

"No, for all of us. That bag could save our lives."

"Or give you a hernia."

Although prepared to face some hardship during our Iberian odyssey, I hadn't expected our trials to begin on a drizzly London morning. On leaving the train Harry had boldly hoisted his holdall onto his right shoulder and set off for the exit, which he reached, just, before dropping the bag onto a bench and rubbing his shoulder.

"I might have overdone the foodstuff."

"Let's get a cab."

"No way. I'll start as I mean to go on. When you two go hiking I'll be coming too." He patted his paunch. "Two miles is nothing."

After another two hundred yards his left shoulder gradually neared the ground and the bag hit the pavement.

"Let's take turns," I said when he'd got his breath back.

"All right." He smiled and took my featherweight rucksack.

I zigzagged to the street corner before my legs gave way. "This is ridiculous, Harry. We must jettison something."

"Ooh, I've just noticed that it's got some little wheels."

"Bastard. Give me my rucksack."

Little wheels there were, but on Harry grabbing the handle, they failed to revolve. I watched him drag the bag for a while, as did everyone we passed. Some of those in suits managed a grimace, though the tourists were openly amused, but when a party of oriental ladies fell in beside him, posing for a photo, he ground to a halt, leered at the camera, and released the handle.

I opened my rucksack and pulled out my sleeping bag. "Put some tins in here and you take this."

He transferred a dozen or so tins – three of *semolina*, for heaven's sake – and shouldered the beastly bag once more.

"Ah, that's much better. It's like bench pressing, you see. Everyone's got their limit."

He reached Russell Square without a break and after leaving the three semolinas next to a bin – he hated the stuff too – we relocated a few tins of mixed veg and made Waterloo Bridge before our next halt.

"Not far now," I said. The drizzle had abated, but Harry's head was as wet as ever. "Look, there's the London Eye, and Big Ben."

Harry only had eyes for the pavement in front of him, but we finally made it, just in time for the Guildford train. By the time we passed through Surbiton he'd stopped hyperventilating and twenty minutes later we hauled the bag off the train and he commenced the final leg.

"I hope he's nearby," he gasped as we passed through the station doors.

"He promised that he would be. Oh my God."

"What?"

"You'd better put that down, Harry."

Directly opposite us, in the car park, a once-white vehicle stood out above the sleek saloons and 4x4s, but not by much. It appeared to be a cross between a decommissioned ice-cream van, a Third World ambulance, and a scale model of one of the earlier motorhomes.

The holdall from hell hit the deck and Harry raised his eyes. "What the f*ck is *that*? No, no, it can't be."

"There's a thin man standing next to it, waving at us."

Harry stood like a statue, so I grasped the handle and dragged the holdall towards Geoff. Harry began to shuffle along behind.

"It looks bigger when you get nearer," I turned to say, before an attack of the giggles made me drop the bag, sit on it, and promptly keel over backwards due to the weight of my rucksack. I looked up to see two faces peering down at me; one large, red and apoplectic, the other with avid eyes, prominent cheekbones and a smile like a crocodile on acid.

"What do you think, lads?" Geoff asked after hauling me upright.

"I think I'll trade that damn holdall in for a rucksack like Jeremy's and the two of us'll entrain for Portsmouth, cross over on the ferry, and go on a *walk*ing tour."

"It's a dinky little thing," I said.

"I'm not getting in it," said Harry.

"Course you are," said Geoff, before grasping the holdall and feistily dragging it over to the toy van.

He dropped the bag and patted the fibreglass bodywork. "The best van on the market, within our price range."

"What *is* it?" I asked. "Is it legal?"

"Of course it is. It's a Bedford Bambi, 1989 model, based on a Suzuki of... er, the same shape, but built in Luton, so it's got Japanese technology and English workmanship, a fine combination."

"Technology isn't a word that springs to mind when you look at it," Harry said.

"I know the Japanese tend to be a bit smaller than us, but is it really made for grownups?" I asked.

"It's a veritable tardis. Come and look inside." He ushered us around to the back, where he opened a narrow door in the middle, before leading the way into our hypothetical home for the next month. I followed, and after passing the cooker and sink, we shuffled between two cushioned benches and seated ourselves on the end of each. When Harry finally managed to get in – sideways – he slowly regained his full height.

"You see, it's bigger than it looks, isn't it?" said our host.

"Hmm," said Harry, a positive sign.

I bounced on the long cushion. "Quite comfy." I looked forward into the cab. "There's the just one thing that I'm not quite sure about, Geoff."

"What?"

"Well, there are two seats up front, and you and I are sitting on what are presumably the two beds."

"Yes, and there's a table we can put up too, just here, between us. It slots into that handy hole."

"That's lovely, Geoff. Oh, look, there's a big man over there glowering down at us. I was never much good at maths, but he doesn't seem to fit into the equation, does he?"

"I've thought it all through, Jeremy," he said gravely, before reaching into a space above the cab and pulling down a roll of blue plastic.

"What that? A body bag?" Harry growled.

"This, my friends, is our third bed, otherwise known as an air mattress, which I purchased yesterday, along with a foot pump. We simple inflate it, insert it into the ample passageway, and our ménage à trois can bed down for the night like three peas in a pod."

"An apt simile," I said.

"I'm not sleeping down there. It's claustrophobic and my shoulders won't fit," said Harry, now seated at the foot of my bench.

"*Or*, we have another alternative. These cushions behind use can be used to make the whole area, bar the cooker and sink, into one big bed. How'd you fancy that?"

"Me and you'll take turns at sleeping on the floor," I said.

"I'm glad I brought my tent," said Harry, who, it must be said, was eyeing our haven with something verging on restrained approval, until he spoilt it by tutting and shaking his head.

"What's up, Harry?" I asked.

"I've just remembered what it looks like from the outside. My God, if anyone from the force saw me in this…"

"Thank goodness we're going abroad," I said.

"Exactly," said Geoff. "In Santander we cast off our inhibitions and take to the road like the three young rogues we used to be." He glanced at us. "Or I used to be. Oh, there's an awning too, that fits on the back, so that's another option."

"Call me a bore, but I must return to my obsession with the number three. I spy only two seats up ahead." I pointed at them. "Where, prey, is the third body going to travel?"

"Oh, back here."

Harry cleared his throat, sounding very much like a policeman.

"Hello, hello, hello," I said.

"Precisely," said the ex-bobby. "Unless the law has changed in the last fourteen months, I believe it is illegal to travel in a vehicle unless secured by a seatbelt."

"I've brought a few bungie cords," Geoff said with a laugh so weak that it could have passed for a sob.

"It's a problem, Geoff," I said.

"We won't be going very fast. The engine's only 970cc."

"Christ, how's that supposed to pull the three of us over mountain passes?" Harry asked.

"It's got gears, and it's designed to carry our weight, just about. Jeremy, I thought you wouldn't mind chilling out back here while we pop down to Portsmouth. It won't matter so much in Spain."

"Why not?"

"We-ell, they're more laid back there, aren't they? I used to smoke dope with a local cop in Jaén."

"Oh, well, if we bump into him we'll be all right then," I said with unavoidable irony.

"He got sacked, for shagging a minor. Honest though, I know from experience that they don't nit-pick like British coppers, present company excepted."

"I'd have thrown the bloody book at anyone riding in the back of a crate like this. No, at the driver, because anyone riding back here would have to be certifiable."

"Well, if we get stopped you just leave the cops to me, and I'll make sure I've always got a fifty euro note handy, or maybe two."

"Just one more question, Geoff. Is it insured?" I asked.

"Insured? Of course it's insured. Do you think I'm some kind of reckless moron or what? I insured it yesterday and all three of us can drive it. Right, let's get this show on the road."

If you'd told me… well, any time before it actually happened, that one day I'd be riding down the A3 lying flat on my face in the back of a miniature camper van, I'd have said you were insane. At first I tried gazing nonchalantly at the roof with my hands behind my head, but soon found it more expedient to turn over and grasp the side of the 'bed' firmly and anchor my foot in between the cushions and the woodwork. It was a long forty-odd miles to the ferry terminal, the whining of the engine accompanied by the droning of Geoff's voice.

"So, I picked her up yesterday at about midday. She's been serviced and the bloke who sold her has great feedback on EBay, so I reckon we won't have any mechanical worries. I then drove to a great big supermarket and stocked up on food. Did you two bother to bring any?"

"A bit," Harry mumbled.

"I also bought three camping chairs and a little table, which are stored in the handy space over the cab."

"Where's the toilet?" I yelled.

"Under the sink. We just pull it out and sit down. I've bought the chemicals, and bog roll, but we'd be best to use the campsite toilets or the great outdoors when possible, using the trowel I bought. Opposite the sink and loo, under the hob and grill, there's a little fridge, now full of food, which is gas powered, though it also runs off the leisure battery, which is fairly new. There was one full bottle of gas and I've bought another, so we'll be all right for a while and can get some more at the campsites."

"You'll have to tell us what we owe you," I said.

"Oh, we'll reckon up after we've sold it. These vans are rare nowadays and I imagine they're quite sought after on the continent, so I might end up sharing money out rather than collecting it."

"Most unlikely. Is there a shower?" asked Harry, causing me to splutter into the cushion.

"Er, no, but there's a sink."

"Hot water?"

"No, but the deposit's full and I've bought a collapsible water container. We could leave that in the sun for a bit and give each other showers with it."

"So I guess we'll be staying at campsites most nights," Harry said.

"Er, some nights, yes, when there's one on our route, but it's no problem to wild camp in Spain. Lots of people do it, especially the Dutch, apparently, who are famed for spending sod all on Spanish soil, apart from on fuel."

"But they'll be in proper vans, won't they?" Harry said.

"Bigger vans, yes, but like Jeremy once said, they cost at least twenty grand. Oh, Jeremy, did you manage to book the ferry?"

I turned my head to one side. "Yes, it was a snip at the price."

"What?" asked the deaf one, so I shouted.

"How much?"

"Oh, just under five hundred quid, nothing really."

"The costs are mounting," Harry wailed.

"I got us a cabin of course, as it's a long… it'll be more comfortable."

"How long does it take?" Harry asked Geoff.

"Well, we set off at about five and arrive at about six."

"Just an hour? Surely not."

"No, not an hour."

"Thirteen?"

"Not a bad idea, the cabin," Geoff said over his shoulder. "Time'll pass quicker."

"Thir*teen*?" Harry repeated.

"Twenty-five, but the ship's so big that you'll hardly know you're on it."

"Shit, you know I'm a bad sailor."

"I've bought some seasickness pills, or anti-seasickness pills, I should say."

"You certainly seem to have thought of everything, Geoff," I said, keen to change the subject.

"One tries." The van juddered to a halt. "This is where one of us gets out."

I peered out of the side window and saw a car park and some trees. "Where are we?"

"Not far off the terminal. One of us ought to go on as a foot passenger, in case they inspect the van and find three of us in it."

"I only printed one ticket, for three men and a van."

"Oh, right. Harry, you're the legal expert. Do you think they'll mind if they find three of us in a two-man van?"

"I don't care. I'm quite happy to be thrown off. Twenty-five flaming hours on a boat. Jeremy, we'll swap round and if they arrest me as an illegal immigrant, or emigrant, so much the better."

We changed places, Harry lay down on the floor atop the uninflated airbed, and we got on board unmolested. It proved to be a solitary journey for me, but we had time for a drink in the lounge before Harry began to feel seasick and Geoff started to suffer from a malady in no way related to sea travel.

"You see," he said with his still full pint. "You can hardly tell we're moving."

"We're scarcely out of the port yet," Harry replied, sucking a pill to maximise its effect.

"So how many miles has our van done?" I asked, planning to take Harry's mind off his future woes for as long as possible.

"Just fifty-four thousand," said Geoff.

"My arse," said Harry.

"It's got a full service history. That was one of my prerequisites."

"Forged, you numpty."

"Nonsense, I'll show it to you."

He extracted the booklet from his effeminate little bag and the stamps and signatures were suspiciously homogenous, few showing any signs that over twenty-five years had elapsed since the first one.

"Dealers love an empty service book," said Harry, before sipping his tonic water.

"He wasn't a dealer. He was a very nice man. She'll get us through Spain without a hitch, you'll see."

"Hitch is the word. That's what we'll be doing before long," said Harry. "I must buy a rucksack as soon as I can."

"What route will we take?" I asked.

Geoff rubbed his hands together. "Well, we'll take our time down through Cantabria, as it's lovely, and then we could maybe have a look at Burgos, a city I always wanted to visit during my years in Spain but never got round to it. Then we have to decide whether we go round Madrid to the east or the west, unless you want to visit it."

"No," I said. "It oughtn't to be that type of trip."

"In that thing the fewer big places we go through the better," said Harry, popping another pill.

"Which is best then, east or west?" I asked Geoff.

"We-ell, each way has its charms. Extremadura, to the west, is a sparsely populated area, with a few nice sierras and huge plains.

"And to the east of Madrid?"

"We'd head from Burgos to... south of there, where I believe it's sparsely populated with a lot of nice sierras and...er, a few plains."

"Have you been to either area?" Harry asked.

"Not exactly, though I've visited many places on google maps; the street view, you know."

"Just where *have* you been in Spain, Geoff?" Harry asked, beginning to look pale and sound irritable.

"To be honest, I was so busy with work and Carmela that I didn't get out of Andalucia much."

"But you know Seville, Cordoba and Granada, I guess," I said.

"Ah, Granada is beautiful! El Alhambra, la Sierra Nevada, marvellous!"

"Have you been there?"

"No, but we bused it down to Almeria once."

Harry snorted.

"What's it like?" I asked.

"Dry."

"Wouldn't it be best to go down the coast?" Harry asked.

"Ugh, no! All those tourists and ugly developments! We must steer clear of all that." He sipped his pint tentatively, also beginning to look a bit peaky.

"There's the seaside though," I said. "You can't beat the seaside. A foray to the coast would be good, somewhere nice like Denia or Javea, which I visited a few years ago with June."

"Hmm, maybe east is best, I guess, as beyond Extremadura there's only Portugal, and there's nothing to see there."

"Lisbon's lovely," I said. "And Sintra and Mafra. June and I spent a week there."

"Have you been to Portugal, Geoff?" Harry asked. I reckoned he only had a couple more questions left in him before he retired to suffer alone and that he meant to make them count.

"No."

"Any other countries?"

"Belgium… and Jersey."

"Some bloody travel expert you are! I wish I'd brought my iPad now, so we could plan ahead."

Before leaving we'd agreed to leave our internet devices behind so that we wouldn't be tempted to use the campsite Wi-Fi to kill time in an unproductive and antisocial way. Geoff had even left his smartphone at home, and Harry didn't have one, so we just had my rather old one for essential use. I'd bought most of the regional Michelin maps though, which indicate the mountains and picturesque roads, so I was sure we'd manage to find the pretty areas.

"Right, I'm off to the cabin," said Harry. "I'll take the bed and you two have the bunks, so you won't disturb me, *if* I manage to get any sleep." He pushed himself to his feet and tottered off.

I finished my pint. "Another one, or shall we go and get a bite to eat?"

Geoff swirled the beer in his glass, then quickly averted his eyes. "I might go up and get some air. I think I've got one of my headaches coming on."

"I didn't know you suffered from headaches, Geoff."

"Oh yes, on and off for years."

"I don't suppose this swell will help. The sea must be a bit choppy."

"Oh, it's nothing to do with the boat, nothing at all."

"Have you done much sailing?"

"Oh yes, to France, the Isle of Man, er… Windermere, you know. Never a problem."

"Maybe it brings on your headaches."

"Hmm."

"Another pint?"

"No ta, it's crap bitter." He pushed his glass away. "I'll just saunter around on deck for a while."

"I'll come with you."

"No, no, get yourself another pint."

"Ha, there's no rush, and if I drink too much I might get a bit queasy." I stood up and smiled down at him. I'd experienced a couple of awful channel crossings in my younger days and knew that I was one of the lucky ones. I took pity on my friend, however, and allowed him to go off alone, but not before suggesting that he took the lower bunk.

"As you wish," he said, before marching boldly to the door.

After another leisurely pint I went up on deck to watch the sunset. There was a sharp breeze, but it was fine, so I ambled around all the walkable area, seeing no sign of Geoff, who must have retired to join Harry in the sickbay.

After a bite to eat I returned to the lounge and decided to have one more drink before going to bed. I reflected on the journey so far and the four weeks which lay ahead of us. After the initial shock I'd begun to see the van in a more positive light. Though ugly as sin and ridiculously underpowered, it did sound fairly smooth and the brakes worked, something I'd already related to June in a text message. The tyres were good too, and I was impressed by Geoff's organisational skills, as we appeared to be all set to head off into the great unknown with everything we required. On finishing my pint I ordered a double whisky nightcap, in order to sleep through the toing and froing of my companions. I was glad that I'd booked a cabin, and gladder still that there was an en suite bathroom.

After another turn on deck I went to the cabin, tried to ignore the sickly, vomitorium-type smell, undressed, and got into bed. Harry was sleeping and Geoff was pretending to, as I heard a few feeble groans before I nodded off.

3

My friends were poor company the next day, which was a pity, as being unable to leave the cabin meant that they missed the glorious sunshine and the sense of camaraderie between the good sailors, of whom there were plenty as the sea wasn't very rough at all. I got chatting to a man of about fifty called Frank who was setting off on a cycle tour. The wiry chap was a veteran of many expeditions and told me that he planned to spend three weeks in the north-west of Spain, before returning to his dental practice in Birmingham.

"What's the north-west like?" I asked him as we sat facing the sun.

"Beautiful. I'll ride through Asturias and the wonderful Picos de Europa mountains, and then into Galicia, which has some amazing roads through huge forests. I'll do a circular tour and end up back in Santander. How about you?"

He was a friendly chap and we had time to kill, so I compressed the essence of what I've told you into a ten minute narrative.

He smiled and scratched his shaven head. "I see. Well, it's nice to have a distant goal. I once rode from the Hook of Holland to Marseilles and then flew back."

"Wow, that sounds good, but, you know, I'm starting to think that a circular tour might be better for us, considering our... means of transport."

"Hmm, you could spend a great month just in the north, but if you do head for Gibraltar, I'd go for the eastern route. Castile and Extremadura have their charms, but they can get monotonous and you'll not find many campsites. I would head roughly towards Murcia, maybe via Cuenca, and then check out the coast south from there, as it's relatively unspoilt. There are loads of spots to stop in motorhomes by the sea, and as it's not the tourist season I doubt the police will move you on. Then I'd drive through the Almeria desert, as it's quite a sight, and head west into the Alpujarras, a lovely valley to the south of the Sierra Nevada."

"Just a sec," I said, fishing a pen and a bit of paper from my jacket pocket. I jotted down what he'd told me. "And after the Alpujarras?"

"Well, you could drive down to the coast from there. Between Motril and Malaga there are some nice places, like Almuñécar and Nerja, and also some pretty mountain villages not far from the coast. From Malaga to Gib it's not so nice – Torremolinos and all that – but if you've got time, go inland and check out Ronda and the other white villages."

I scribbled away gratefully. "You're a mine of information, Frank."

"I've been coming to Spain every other year since living in Granada for eighteen months after graduating. It's a great country, and brilliant for cycling."

I pictured Geoff, not writhing and moaning in his bed due to his headache, but waxing lyrical in Jaén with Carmela and his many Spanish friends. "Did you learn the language when you lived here?"

"Pretty much. I studied hard and practised a lot."

"And do you still speak it well now?"

"Oh, I get by, but I've lost a lot over the years, despite my visits. Ha, twenty-eight years is a long time! Why do you ask, Jeremy?"

"Oh, one of my pals lived there too, almost as long ago, and I was wondering if his Spanish would still be OK."

"Has he visited often since then?"

"No, not at all."

"Then unless he's one of those really gifted linguists, I imagine he'll have forgotten most of it, though he'll still know the basics, I guess."

"Hmm, interesting. Well, I'd better go and see how they are."

"OK, I'll look out for you when we disembark. I'm intrigued about that van of yours."

"You can't miss it. There'll be nothing else like it."

About an hour before our arrival time I began to rouse my convalescing comrades.

"How are you feeling, Harry?"

He sat up and grimaced bravely. "I no longer wish to die, like last night. I haven't felt so bad for the last few hours, but I didn't want to risk moving; you know, if it's not broken…"

"Well, you've certainly begun your diet with a vengeance."

"I feel purged," he said as his feet hit the floor.

"How's that head of yours, Geoff?" I asked the shrouded figure in the bottom bunk.

"A bit better, thanks. That's the worst migraine I've ever had."

"It must have been," said Harry. "You were puking up more than me."

"Bad migraines can have that effect." I winked at Harry. "Do you feel like going up to watch us sail into port?"

"Yep," said Harry. "I've missed too much already and as it's the last time I'm ever going on a ship, I'd better make the most of it."

"Geoff?"

"Yes, I'll be up in a jiffy."

It was wonderful to steam into the bay past a huge palace and golden sand dunes, and the city itself looked splendid in the afternoon sun. Neither Harry nor Geoff seemed too much the worse for wear – I think they'd just been too wary to get up – and I asked them if they fancied exploring Santander.

"Then we could park up for the night near a beach somewhere. A very well-informed bloke I met says the police don't usually mind."

"Oh, I think we should push on, don't you?" said Geoff. "We've many a mile to cover and it'd be good to get on the road."

"It'll be dark in three hours," I countered.

"It looks like a fine place, Jeremy, but I'd prefer to get used to being in the van without too many folk around," said Harry. "I'm still not in the mood for having the piss ripped out of me."

"Are you ever?" asked Geoff.

"All right then, but let's go for the eastern route. The bloke gave me a few pointers as to where to head and he knows Spain like the back of his hand," I said, intending to elaborate at a later date, as Geoff would need to be hoodwinked into believing that he'd planned the route himself. "I've got the map ready."

"I've brought my satnav," said Geoff.

"I thought we weren't doing technology on this trip?"

"Satnavs stink," said Harry. "That bloody oining voice gets on my wick."

"They're good in cities," said Geoff.

"OK, well, use it to get us out of this one, then stash it away," said Harry curtly.

I decided to disembark on foot, rather than risking the wrath of the customs men, who might think the one in the back was being people-smuggled. I passed through passport control and studied the map as I waited for our chariot to leave the terminal. A few motorbikes trundled past first, then some cars, followed by some stunning motorhomes. There was one of those old VW campers too, with an engine that sounded a bit like Geoff's Harley Davidson, which is ancient, but none of these vehicles prepared me for the first sight of our Bedford Bambi.

The name Bambi evokes something sleek and gazelle-like and I hope whoever came up with the name for that sandwich box on wheels was sacked on the spot. I was preparing to hurl myself into its nether regions as it passed by when Frank appeared, pushing his well-laden bike along the pavement.

"That's it, just coming," I said, pointing down the road.

"Where?"

"Behind that big blue one."

"F*ck me," he said, the first time I'd heard him swear.

"Gibraltar here we come."

"Oh, well. It's the journey that counts, not the conveyance. I'm sure you'll enjoy yourselves," he said, before patting me softly – perhaps pityingly – on the shoulder and pushing off.

"You too," I said, before falling in behind the crawling van and hopping inside. As I shut the door I peered through the little window and saw three people seated in the cab of a plush motorhome, all of them laughing hysterically. A sign of things to come, I thought as I sat on the bench and gripped the side of Harry's seat, a fairly stable way to ride, I soon discovered, and away from the side window.

"Have you set the satnav?" I asked Geoff.

"No, I don't know where we're going yet. I'll pull over here."

I looked at the map. "I think we ought to head for a place called Solares."

"So-la-res. In Spanish you pronounce every letter and you accentuate the second-to-last syllable, unless there's an accent that indicates otherwise."

"Right," I said, impressed. Maybe Geoff was one of those natural linguists who Frank had mentioned.

The satnav lady seemed happy with that and we were soon heading past the docks on a dual-carriageway. Goodbye, Santander, I thought, though I too was glad to hit the open road. Although it was best for me to keep out of sight, I couldn't help peering out of the window, mainly to find out what the intermittent pipping was all about. The road was busy and as we were hogging the slow lane, the fast lane soon became pretty pedestrian too, enabling the motorists to feast their eyes on Bambi, as we soon began to refer to the van, more through mockery than affection. We were the cause of the pipping, of course, but on the whole they weren't pips of anger or frustration, as most of the faces I spotted were suffused with mirth, and when one van passenger spotted me, he doubled up with laughter, causing the driver to lean over, look and swerve, so I ducked and resumed my perch near the front.

"Will this thing not go a bit faster?" I asked. "There are about six lorries behind us."

"Fifty seems to be about tops, unless I really push her."

"No, don't do that. I'll be glad to get off this road."

"So will I," Harry grunted. "The next bugger who laughs at me will get this bloody satnav through his windscreen. Christ, I thought I was badly off on the boat, but this is purgatory."

"Just smile back at them," said Geoff. "That's what I do."

"You keep your eyes on the road. This thing's about as stable as a… as a…"

"Toaster on wheels?" I ventured.

"Yes, except a toaster's more powerful. Oh, thank God she's telling us to turn off," Harry said, pointing to the slip road up ahead.

Solares looked like a pleasant little town and a couple of coaches implied that it attracted tourists, so I suggested that we park up and take a look around.

"We've only done ten miles," said Geoff after pulling over. "And look, there are blocks of flat."

"Nice ones, and people have to live somewhere."

"Oh, let's get right away from the hustle and bustle."

Just then a couple of slaps on the side of the van heralded the arrival of a posse of kids who proceeded to circle Bambi and make what I assumed to be derisive comments. Maybe they imagined that such a feeble vehicle would be inhabited by equally feeble folk, but when Harry jumped down and yelled, "Bugger off, you little sods," off they buggered, double quick.

"Jeremy, tell me the name of the next place to the south of here," Geoff said.

"Er... Liérganes," I attempted to say.

"Is there an accent?"

"Yes, above the 'e'."

"Then that would be Liérganes," he said in an odd, mumbling voice. "Hmm, the satnav says we have to get back on the dual-carriageway."

"No, no, no. That's the trouble with satnavs. They don't like little roads and there's one that takes us straight there. Turn left just ahead. We go around the town and south for about five miles. It's much further her way."

"Are you sure?"

"Positive," I said, crossing my fingers. If I could get this one right there was a chance that we'd have heard the last of that cold, robotic voice, so when we passed a large park and a smart two-storey building with flags outside – probably the town hall – I was relieved to see a signpost to our destination. I'd thought it a shame to leave yet another place unexplored, but when we left the pretty hamlet of Hermosa behind and began to climb into the hills, I became riveted by the scenery. This wasn't my idea of Spain at all, as the lush fields and woods were just like English countryside, though there were far fewer drystone walls.

I got a really good view of it all too, as on rounding a hairpin bend our speed slowed to about ten miles an hour.

"Is there something wrong?" I asked Geoff.

"No, I'm letting Bambi dictate the speed and she prefers second gear. Remind me to check the oil and water when we stop for the night."

"Is she overheating?"

"Nope, not if I let her take her time."

"Should I get out and walk?" asked Harry. "Like in the good old days of horses and carts."

"No need. I think that's the top just ahead."

Though pleased with Geoff's prudence, I was soon wondering why we were going down the other side at a similar speed, so I asked him.

"This is her first downhill and I want to see how she behaves on the bends… not too bad, I think. She looks top-heavy, but she isn't really. Right, hold on tight back there, Jeremy."

"Why?" I asked, grasping Harry's seat.

The answer was what I think was intended to be an emergency stop, and no more than forty yards later we had come to a halt on the empty road.

"Hmm, not bad," said our driver.

"Did you brake hard?" asked Harry.

"Foot to the floor. There's a lot of weight on board," he said, grasping Harry's thigh.

"Get off!"

"We'll have to take it *very* steady down proper hills. Bear that in mind when you're driving, both of you."

"I'm not driving this heap," said Harry.

"That's all right, but you'll have to do a double turn in the back."

"I'll drive," I said. "It's a bit weird sitting sideways all the time. I'm starting to feel a bit seasick."

"I'll drive too," said Harry.

"It's quite fun, really. Do you remember that 2CV I used to have?"

"Oh, yes," I said, remembering the time when he'd driven us both up to Kendal in it to see the latest in a long line of rental properties, the one he'd shared with the huge lizard for a while.

"Well, it's a bit like driving that. You haven't got much horsepower to play with, so you have to use the gears and take your time."

"Just how far are we going to drive altogether?" Harry asked.

"Well, it's six hundred and odd miles straight there, so I guess we'll end up doing eight, maybe nine hundred."

"That's only about thirty a day," I said. "I'm sure we can manage that, though I suppose we'll do longer drives some days and stay in one place for a while now and then," I said hopefully, before spotting the village up ahead. "This looks nice. Shall we stop here for the night?"

"We've only done half our daily quota," said Geoff.

"Oh, bollocks, I want a beer," said Harry. "I noticed there are none in the fridge."

"No room for luxuries in there. Are you sure it's worth stopping here?"

"Geoff, it's a lovely village nestled in a wooded valley. Those people there look like tourists. If it's not worth stopping here, where *do* we stop? It's about time we made contact with the natives, too. I haven't heard a word of Spanish yet."

"Except those bloody kids," said Harry.

"Oh, all right, a quick beer. Let's have a look down here," Geoff said as he turned left onto a charming street of red-tiled stone houses with wooden balconies that looked like they'd had more than a bob or two spent on them.

On reaching a quaint little square we parked next to some cars on the cobbles in the middle and jumped out to stretch our legs.

"*Very* chocolate boxy, I must say," said Geoff.

"Let's find a bar," said Harry.

"Ask that lady, Geoff," I said.

He approached a drably dressed woman of about sixty who appeared to be transfixed by Bambi, judging by her slack-jawed stare. Geoff spoke to her quickly in that funny voice of his and she transferred her attentions to him, though her expression didn't alter much. Geoff spoke again, more slowly and succinctly, upon which the woman closed her mouth and nodded slowly, but offered up no information. He then said, "Un bar, por favor," which even I understood, and so did she, as we were soon walking back the way we'd come, to a hostelry she'd pointed in the rough direction of.

"She didn't seem to understand you," Harry said as we walked in single file along the narrow pavement.

"I'm not sure she was right in the head," he replied. "Did you see the way she stood looking at the van?"

"She's not the first to be taken that way. Here we are," I said as we reached a square stone edifice with a striking green, glazed, wooden balcony and, more importantly, a few tables outside. We sat down and waited for someone to appear.

"Beer for me," Harry said to Geoff.

"Shouldn't you eat something first, after being so ill?" I asked.

"My stomach lining will appreciate the feeling of something familiar," he said.

"They won't have bitter," Geoff said.

"I wouldn't want one. Cold lager on holiday, bitter at home."

"I'll have one too," I said.

When the young waiter came out I expected Geoff to say, "Tres cervezas, por favor," as I would have done, but instead he smiled and launched into a speedy, marble-mouthed monologue, which received a brief response.

"Qué?" said the lad politely, and nothing more.

Geoff tried again, a bit more slowly and briefly, causing him to nod, smile, and raise his pen and pad in the air.

"Tres cervezas, por favor," I said, upon which he said OK, snapped his pad shut, and strode back inside.

I looked over Harry's head at the modern building opposite, while Harry looked straight at Geoff.

"Er, it appears that your Spanish might be a little rusty, Geoff," he said.

"Oh, they don't speak the same up here in the north," he said with a dismissive wave.

"No-one's said anything to you yet. They just nod or stare."

"Hmm, my accent's pure Andaluz, you see. We miss letters off down there and sort of run the words together. I might have to speak more… academic Spanish to these yokels."

"Quite," Harry said.

Then something funny happened. When the lad returned with our bottles and glasses on a tray, he appeared to have mustered up the courage to try out his very passable English, as he asked us if we were staying in the village for long. Before Geoff could reply in Spanish I told him about our proposed journey, glad that Bambi was out of sight.

"Ah, Gibraltar. I have been there a lot. I'm from Algeciras, a town very near there. I come to work here every summer. Call me if you need anything else," he said, before going back inside.

As Geoff appeared to grow smaller in his chair, I was happy to let the matter rest there, but Harry cleared his throat in that inimitable way of his and I knew Geoff was in for it. Before speaking, however, Harry poured out and drank off half of his beer, while Geoff took a quick slug from his bottle, smiled, and twiddled his thumbs.

"Algeciras. That must be in Andalucia then," said Harry.

"Yes, in the province of Cádiz. Andalucia's a big place, you see, and every province has its own accent. I can do a Cádiz accent for you, if you like. It's very different."

"Oh, come off it, Geoff!" he said with a laugh. "You've forgotten your Spanish and that's all there is to it."

"Nonsense, I'm just a bit… rusty."

"Completely seized up, I'd say. Jeremy, you can speak a bit. We'll just have to rely on you."

Geoff went red as he poured out his beer, though the knuckles around the bottle turned white. While Harry is quick-tempered, Geoff is more prone to sulking, so, wishing to avoid a tense first evening, I strove to find the right conciliatory words.

"I think what's happened is this, Geoff. I reckon all your Spanish has lain latent in your brain for so long that when you come to use it, it doesn't come out quite the way it should. Maybe you need to ease your way back into it. You know, speak slowly and stick to basics until it comes back of its own accord."

"Hmm."

"What did you say to the waiter, anyway?"

"I just said what a lovely village it was and that we had come over on the ferry and were planning to drive through Spain in our motorhome."

"Motor-hovel," said Harry.

"Try saying something more straightforward to the lad when he comes out again."

"No, he's spoken to us in English now and spoilt it. Let's move on and I'll bear in mind what you've said. It has been a long time, after all."

"Exactly. It'll be going dark quite soon. Shall we ask him if there's a campsite nearby?"

"Well, we could just drive on and try to find a place–"

"Definitely," Harry interrupted. "It'll be hard enough to get used to sleeping in that thing as it is, and I'll need a shower at some point. Hello there!" he boomed at the doorway. "Is there a campsite near here?" he asked the speedy waiter.

"There is a good one in La Pedrosa, about fifteen kilometres to the south."

"Thanks. Then that's where we'll go, eh, Geoff?"

"OK," he replied, somewhat mollified by my explanation of his execrable Spanish. "La cuenta, por favor," he said slowly.

"Cuatro cincuenta."

"Here you are. Keep the change, and thanks a lot. We'll come back again one day," Geoff told us he said in Spanish, and I believed him as the lad seemed to understand this time.

"Buen viaje," were his parting words, and we headed back down the street to Bambi, who seemed more of an eyesore than ever, parked betwixt those charming stone houses.

Although the light was fading fast we could still appreciate the marvellous countryside as I drove Bambi along the verdant valley where trees towered above us by the roadside. The road was narrow but well-surfaced and I soon got used to the peculiarities of our van, which didn't handle as badly as I'd expected, though I took every bend with great care, fearful that an oncoming vehicle might crush us to death, as I felt quite vulnerable in that small, bonnet-less cab. I spotted the river now and then, but I was concentrating too hard to appreciate it.

"It's lovely round here," I said. "We don't want to be rushing off before we've enjoyed it thoroughly."

"All Cantabria's like this," said Geoff from the back.

"Yes, but if I remember rightly it's a narrow province. We ought to stick around tomorrow and explore a bit."

"Well, I don't know…"

"We'll vote, which means we're staying," said Harry.

"Let's see what the campsite looks like," I said, as I wanted Geoff to fully recover his high spirits before we arrived. We passed through a few hamlets which had tourism and second homes written all over them, before crawling down a narrow lane to the campsite in the dying light. We jumped down and breathed in the fresh evening air, reminiscent of the Lake District. A slim young lady came out to greet us and Geoff, in very few words, told her that we'd like to camp for the night. As I could already see that the place was almost empty, there was no need to insist on a second night just then, as democracy would ensure that Geoff's mile-eating mania would be put on hold for a while.

She led us over to a grass pitch and pointed to a socket, before wishing us buenas noches.

"Cuánto es?" I asked.

"Mañana," she replied.

"Is there a bar?" Harry said in perfect English.

"Hmm, yes, but I close now. Few people, you see," she said, pointing to the only two tents within view.

"Can we buy some beers, to take away?" Harry asked.

"Of course. Come with me. Oh, and I will show you the bathrooms," she said, clearly keen to be off.

As we approached the bar – actually a bona fide restaurant – situated in the square stone house near the entrance, she seemed to see Bambi for the first time. Her mouth didn't fall open, which was something, but she paused to admire the vehicle that if she worked there for fifty years she might never see again.

"You have tents, no?"

"No, we sleep inside," I said.

Her olive brow ruffled and she stifled a smile.

"There are three beds," Harry said, his deep voice positively cavernous, because, he told us later, he feared she might think we were bum-chums – his words, not mine. "And we've got a tent, if we find we need it."

"And an awning," I said, which I'd forgotten about until then.

Harry purchased twelve bottles of beer and assured her he would return *all* the empties the following morning – as if gay blokes didn't drink – and we said our final farewells, before I moved Bambi onto our first ever pitch.

"Did you not fancy talking to her?" Harry asked Geoff.

"Not once you started speaking English. Someone'll always speak it on campsites and it breaks the spell."

"What spell?" I asked.

"I don't know, the linguistic spell. Back in Jaén hardly anyone spoke English, least of all the students, so it was easy to learn Spanish, but down on the coast they were always keen to speak it. I found that there was usually a brief linguistic battle and whoever came out on top got to carry on in the language of their choice. Of course, if you blurt out something in English like that, it's game over right away," he said, but not in a sulky way.

"We'll bear that in mind," I said. "I'd like to improve my Spanish a bit too, though I know very little."

"I just wanted the beer, and I got it," Harry said, pulling a Swiss Army knife from his pocket and opening three. "They're cold too."

"Great, let's sort things out while we drink," I said, as night was falling rapidly.

Sorting things out turned out to consist of hooking up the electric and taking the little table and three chairs outside, as there was neither time nor necessity to attempt to set up the awning. When I went in to store the remaining bottles in the fridge, I saw that Harry was beginning to unpack his colossal holdall.

"I wouldn't do that, if I were you," I said.

"Why not?"

"Well, if we all unpack, or if just you unpack, where are we going to sleep?"

"Hmm, good point."

"I think our bags will have to double as our wardrobes."

We extracted the thirty or so tins of food from his bag and mine, and stashed them in a drawer under one of the benches, along with a few clothes to stop them rattling. None of us felt like cooking or heating anything up just then, so we made do with bread, cheese, cold meat and fruit for our first ever camping meal together. Before I settled down I pulled down the airbed and pumped it up. The less I thought about bedding down for the night, the happier I felt.

"Well, this *is* nice," said Geoff after his second beer. With our jackets on it was pleasant to sit and listen to the faint murmur of the stream and breathe in the fragrant night air.

"Yes, this is the life," said Harry, before belching softly. "Why don't we just stay here for a month?"

"Because we have a mission," I said, feeling in no mood for mutiny. "We'll stay another night and then make tracks. Remember that everywhere we visit we can always come back to another time. I still can't quite believe I've retired."

"Me neither," said Harry. "But being here makes me appreciate it more. There are things to do and places to see before we snuff it."

"I wish I'd retired," said Geoff softly.

"Ha, don't wish your life away," I said.

"Though there'll be no handsome pension for me, I'm afraid."

Harry opened three more bottles. "What you want to do is find something you like doing and stick to it."

"I wish."

"You're a bright bloke, Geoff," I said. "Instead of doing jobs that you hate, you ought to set up some kind of business."

He sat up straighter in his chair. "I'd like that, and I've got tons of ideas, but I lack the backing, though I guess my aunt's money is a start."

In the dim light from the electric lantern I could see Harry squirm in his camp chair, but I was feeling benevolent enough to pursue the subject.

"What would you do and where would you do it?"

"Oh, I can turn my hand to anything, but I'd love to come back to live in Spain. It's only out first day, but I wish I'd never left. While we're travelling I'll see if I get any definite ideas."

"You do that, and Harry and me will think on it too. It'd be nice to have you in Spain, so we could come and visit, wouldn't it, Harry?"

"It'd be nice to have him in Spain, yes," he said with a grin. "I'll put my thinking cap on, but not just now. Let's just chill out and enjoy this."

"Carpe diem," I said, stretching my legs.

While drinking our last beer we all began to wilt and sleeping in the van no longer seemed like an impending ordeal.

"I'll take the floor tonight," I said. "I'm so knackered that I don't care where I sleep."

"We can try the awning tomorrow," said Geoff.

"I'm off now. G'night gents," said Harry.

I left them both to stash the superfluous cushions and settle down before partially undressing outside. I then slotted myself between them on the airbed and slipped into my bag. The last sound I heard was Harry's gentle snoring.

4

"Bloody hell, you snore like hell, Harry," was the second sound I heard the following morning, after the chirping of birds.

"I didn't hear him," I said, rising from my coffin-like berth.

"Hmm, I'm a light sleeper, as my brain never stops. We *must* put the awning up today and either me or Harry can sleep in it."

"It might be chilly sleeping out here," I said from the open door. "It's after eight now and still pretty nippy."

"Oh, my sleeping bag's designed for polar expeditions," Geoff said.

"So how come you're not drenched in sweat, Captain Scott?" Harry muttered, still cocooned in his cheap-looking red bag.

"Because I left it unzipped, Amundsen."

"How are the beds?" I asked. "The airbed was fine."

"A tad short and narrow for me, but not too bad," said Harry. "What's for breakfast?"

"There are three types of cereals and there's some bread left."

"Is there a toaster?"

"A grill, under the hob, but it doesn't work."

"Did that very nice man who sold you the van tell you that?" Harry asked.

"Yes, which proves how honest he was. I'll put the kettle on. Tea or coffee?"

We both requested tea.

"Oh."

"What?" I asked.

"There are only two mugs, and… hmm, there seem to be two of everything. The chap did say that he and his wife used the van for years, so I guess there were no kids."

"Stands to reason, using this thing," said Harry.

"Perhaps they'll sell us what we need at the campsite bar," I said.

"Maybe we ought to have breakfast there first, before we ask," said Harry. "I fancy a proper coffee anyway."

Our hostess was quite right to have wished to get away the evening before, as the bar was well and truly open when we arrived, though we were the first customers. Geoff commented – in slow, clear Spanish – that it was very considerate of her to open so early when there were so few campers.

"Oh, I will have to get used to it. It will be busy soon, until September," she replied in English, which seemed to prove Geoff's linguistic hegemony theory correct, so he clamped his mouth shut and left us to order the croissants and coffee, there being no full English breakfast on offer.

"We shouldn't make a habit of this," Geoff said as we munched away.

"Of what?" I asked.

"Of eating out all the time. We don't want to end up being like those useless campers who can't cook for themselves."

"Why not?" Harry asked.

"Because we ought to be more self-sufficient."

"Why? Spain's cheap."

"That's not the point."

"We're only having a bit of breakfast," I said. "It's not even a proper meal. I'm sure we'll be cooking plenty of those."

Just then the girl brought our second coffees and croissants, and more butter and jam. "Today is Friday, so tonight the restaurant will be open," she said. "Our chef is very good, so many local people come at the weekend."

"Local people?" I asked, as I'd seen the menu and there were some dear items on it.

"Well, mainly people from Santander who have houses around here."

"Are there any real local people left?" I asked, thinking about the villages in the Lake District and the Yorkshire Dales, where even a small cottage costs an arm and both legs.

"Some."

"Are you local?" Geoff asked, her slim figure and pretty face overriding his aversion to speaking English to a Spaniard.

"No, but I stay with a local family, from March to October. I'm from a village in Albacete, but there is no work there. Some of my friends have gone to work in England."

"That's interesting," said Geoff, smiling broadly and attempting to dazzle her with his piercing eyes. "Have you time to sit down with us and chat for a while?"

Her brown eyes opened almost as wide as his and she surveyed the empty bar. "No thanks, I have much to do."

"What a shame," he said, rather unctuously. "Maybe–"

"Tell me," I interjected. "Could you sell us a mug, a plate and a bowl, please?"

"And a knife, fork and spoon," added Harry. "We're short, you see."

"Ha, I can give them to you," she said, looking from Harry to me and avoiding Geoff's fluttering eyelids.

"I tell you, if you hadn't cut me off I'd have been having a drink with her later, and who knows what else," Geoff protested as we returned to Bambi with our booty.

"Geoff, she's about thirty years younger than you," I laughed.

"I don't mind. I'm not ageist. Young ladies prefer experienced men. Did you not see the way she looked at me?"

"I saw the way she looked away from you," said Harry.

"Just playing hard to get. I admire reticence in a woman."

"Don't be so bloody daft, you've no chance."

"I'll woo her tonight, you'll see."

"I was planning to invite you two to dinner there, but if you act the goat I'll be eating up quick and leaving you to pay. Harry's right. You sometimes forget how old you are, Geoff."

"Ha, have you forgotten Denise already," he said, referring to a woman he'd courted a couple of years ago.

"She was about thirty and not exactly a stunner," Harry said.

"And not very bright, either," I added.

"And she limped, even before she met you," Harry concluded.

"Denise was a stopgap. Anyway, what are we going to do today?"

"I think we ought to put up the awning and then go for a good walk," I said.

"I'm up for that," said Harry, bending down and pawing the air a few inches above his toes.

"Right, let's get it up pronto and shoot off," said Geoff, before leaping inside.

We unrolled the faded blue awning which hadn't been aired for a while. Within it there were a few dusty poles, rusty pegs and the remains of a roll of duct tape.

"That might come in handy one day," Geoff said.

"It'll come in handy right now," said Harry as he spread the old thing out. "It's rotten and falling to bits. What did the very nice man say about it, Geoff?"

"He just told me it was stashed above the cab. Still, it was good of him to supply the tape."

We decided to erect the decrepit appendage first and repair it *in situ*. The poles were sound, but the guy lines felt brittle. As we tensed the third one the first one snapped, so Harry tied a knot and tried again. The fourth and final one caused the second one to snap, so Harry tied that, which was too much for the third.

"Maybe that besotted girl will have some spare ones lying about. I'll go and ask her," Geoff said, spinning round.

"Wait!" I cried. "Come over here and look at it."

They joined me ten yards from the side of the van and together we surveyed the aesthetic effect of the torn, sagging pavilion.

"It won't do, will it?" I said.

"We'll look like a trio of starving tinkers," said Harry.

"I doubt she'll join me in there," said Geoff.

"Let's chuck it. I fancy using my tent tonight anyway," said Harry.

"I doubt your sleeping bag will keep you warm enough. I'll take the tent tonight, if you like," said Geoff, still dreaming about the unlikeliest coupling since Charles and Oona Chaplin, but of course he'd been a bit wealthier than Geoff.

I started towards the bar. "Take that monstrosity down while I go and see if I can buy some bread for our butties," I said, quickening my pace before Geoff could protest.

She was kind enough to sell me two long, crisp baguettes for a pittance, before asking me how many more nights we were planning to stay.

"Just tonight, if that's OK."

"That's fine. Tomorrow a large group of scouts will arrive, so it will become very noisy."

I then asked her if she enjoyed her job and we ended up chatting for a while. Her name was Marta and she'd studied economics at university in Madrid, but as there were no jobs in Spain and she hadn't fancied going abroad, she'd landed this job and was here for her second season. On the whole she enjoyed it more than she'd expected and loved living in such wonderful countryside. She had already taken a kayak instructor course and planned to become a climbing instructor too.

"I never thought of having a career in this sector, but in Spain one must adapt to circumstances. Maybe one day I will manage an outdoor activity centre, or some similar venture," she said, before suggesting a good walking route and asking if we were going to dine in the restaurant that evening.

"Yes, if that's all right."

"Of course. I will reserve you that table by the window."

I thanked her and was going to warn her about Geoff's potentially bizarre behaviour when her open, intelligent face caused me to change tack and take her into my confidence. I made a conservatively mischievous suggestion regarding her response to Geoff's inevitable advances, but she made a much better one.

"Ha, it will make the evening more interesting," she concluded, and I heartily agreed.

"Took you long enough," said Geoff when I'd placed the bread on the camping table where he was cutting cheese.

"Just having a chinwag with Marta. Charming girl. To be honest, she makes me wish I were thirty years younger, and not married, of course."

"Dream on, old-timer. Tonight you're going to eat your words about me being past it. Who knows, I might end up staying on with Marta and becoming her summer sex slave. I'm glad you told me her name. I'll probably knock up a poem or two while we're out walking… There, three succulent cheese and spam bocadillos."

"Did you buy some tinfoil?" I asked.

"Er, no."

"Clingfilm?" asked Harry.

"Tampoco, meaning neither."

I clambered inside and dug a clean plastic bag out of my rucksack. Geoff put the sandwiches in and tied a knot. Harry said we'd better take plenty of water, as it promised to be a warm day, despite the cloud cover. It transpired that we had neither water bottles nor a knapsack to carry our repast, so the three of us stood looking at the bag for a while.

"We must make a list for when we pass through a big town," I said.

"But what'll we do now?" Geoff asked.

By way of reply Harry bounded into Bambi, making her squeak and shudder, before returning with a tetra-brik of orange juice.

"I'll carry this, you take turns with the bag. Come on, my exercise regime starts right now."

A motley trio we must have appeared as we crossed the river and headed off up a steep lane paved with crumbling concrete, but as there wasn't a soul around it didn't matter. Harry headed uphill at an ambitious pace, casually tossing the orange juice from hand to hand, but by the time we reached a battered old church – after about a hundred yards – he began to puff and pant.

"Take it easy, Harry. I believe it's quite a long climb to the top. We must pace ourselves."

"I could waltz up this little hill, but I'm saving my strength for tonight," said Geoff.

I set a very moderate pace, so as not to discourage Harry, and feasted my eyes on the variety of trees and bushes around us. On previous visits to Spain I'd seen little more than pine trees, but there in Cantabria oak and beech trees predominated, along with a couple of others that I couldn't name, as I'm no dendrologist, or tree-expert. Looking up, I spotted a kestrel hovering, and wished I'd packed my binoculars.

"Don't worry about the clouds, Jeremy," Geoff said. "They're not the rain-bearing type."

"I was looking at the kestrel."

"Oh… oh, that's a peregrine falcon, I think."

I'm no ornithologist either, but I knew it was a kestrel due to its longer tail. It's useless to argue with Geoff about things like that without an expert arbitrator present, however, and I preferred to talk about the type of bird that he's most fond of.

"Do you really, truly think that Marta fancies you, Geoff?"

"I'm not a hundred percent, but my sixth sense tells me that I'm in with a shout. She might be an orphan, or have lost her dad at an early age, so she's subconsciously seeking a father figure. I think it was a bit like that with Denise."

"Denise was desperate… simple as that," Harry managed to say between gasps. "Anything… with a prick."

"Maybe you think she's keen because she's just so pleasant," I said. "I mean, when I was chatting to her I had an inkling that she liked me too. Perhaps Spanish girls are just more open."

"Ha, all's fair in love and war, grandad," he said, which I didn't mind because I am one.

Onwards and upwards we plodded along the lane, past imposing cliffs and lush pastures where black and white cattle grazed. I'd already forgotten Marta's route, so I decided to lead them up to the top of what looked like a mountain pass, before heading back down again. In England we'd have passed numerous footpath signs by then, but I'd seen none, so I guessed that rights to roam might not be so liberal in Cantabria. The scenery became ever wilder and really did remind me of the Lake District, and those non-rain-bearing clouds rang a bell too.

"Are you sure it's not going to rain, Geoff?"

"Nah, in my two years in Spain it only rained a few times. Those clouds'll pass, they always do."

"It looks like it's going to piss it down to me," said Harry, stopping for a breather.

After what seemed like about three miles but probably wasn't, we reached the summit and were treated to the curious sight of a sculpture of a beige cow surrounded by wooden fencing. There was a bench and a picnic table within the small, somewhat bizarre compound, so after taking in the panoramic views we sat on the bench and ate our butties. Either we were high up, or the clouds were very low, and as I tilted my head to take a swig of orange juice a fat drop fell on my forehead.

"It's starting to rain," I said.

"Nonsense," said Geoff.

"Pit-pat," said the drops.

"Shit," said Harry. "We're going to get a right soaking."

"I'll put waterproof jackets on my mental shopping list," I said.

"*I've* got one, in my bag," said Geoff.

"You'd better nip back and get it then," said Harry.

"I could jog back in half an hour."

Geoff stuck with us though, as we descended the lane in the pouring rain, and apart from my squelchy walking shoes I found the experience invigorating, as it wasn't cold, but Bambi was still a welcome sight when we entered the campsite.

"I never thought I'd be glad to see that thing," said Harry, wiping the rain from his brow and putting on a final spurt across the grass.

"Now we know why it's so green around here," I said.

"It'll soon pass," said Geoff as we queued up to file into the van.

Bambi's narrow aisle became a bit crowded as we struggled out of our clothes, and after sharing a bath towel we each began to extract fresh underclothes from our bags. In baggy white y-fronts and a black Judas Priest t-shirt, Harry lay down on the right-hand bench and sighed with relief.

"I enjoyed that hike, though I might pay for it tomorrow."

As Geoff was still rooting for clothes, I stretched out on the other bench. "You did well, Harry. We'll try to walk every day."

"Hey, where am I supposed to sit?" asked the skinny one, now dressed in scarlet boxer shorts and a black fleece top.

"Put the tent up," said Harry. "You've claimed it for tonight."

We reached the restaurant about two hours before our scheduled dinner time, as after an afternoon in the van with the rain drumming on the roof we were ready for a change of scene. The campsite was a quagmire and I didn't envy the scouts who would arrive on the morrow, though by seven, as we picked our way along the puddled track, the rain had begun to abate. In the end we'd taken turns at stretching out and we'd passed the time reading and chatting. I hadn't mentioned Marta again, so when she patted my arm as she greeted us Geoff's eyes looked like two giant blue and white marbles.

"Shall I get you some drinks first, Jeremy? It's a little early to eat."

"Beers all round?" I asked a thirsty Harry and a perplexed Geoff.

While we drank, the restaurant slowly began to fill, with mainly affluent-looking Spanish families and a couple who I knew to be Dutch but Geoff insisted were Germans. Marta was kept busy but never lost an opportunity to beam at me as she floated around, looking divine in a close-fitting black top and blue jeans which showed off the svelte figure that Geoff still planned to undress, as he was undismayed by the state of affairs.

"That is *such* a typical tactic," he said, shaking his head and chuckling.

"What's that, Geoff?" I asked as I returned one of Marta's sweet smiles.

"Well, she's making a point of not looking at me, while smiling like a Cheshire cat at you two. Talk about playing hard to get!"

"She's not smiling at me. I think she's got the hots for Jeremy," said Harry, who I'd taken into my confidence when Geoff had nipped to the loo. "I'll pop back and put the tent up for you after dinner, if you like, Jeremy. At your age you can't miss an opportunity like this, and June will never find out, will she Geoff?"

"What nonsense," he sneered.

"Thanks, Harry, but I'll probably end up making love to her in here, on the floor," I said in a matter-of-fact way after Marta brushed past me, though there was plenty of room between our table and the next.

"There's something funny going on here," said Geoff with furrowed brow and slit-like eyes. "You haven't... you haven't given her some money, have you?"

"Ha, what an idea! Who can explain the chemistry of human attraction? I must say I'm enjoying her attentions, but I shan't be doing anything about it. This means something to me, you see," I said, fingering my wedding ring fondly, which had the effect I expected.

"What? Are you mad? To let slip an opportunity like that is a sin. Let's order dinner and see how things develop. I still think it's part of her strategy to get me in the sack, but if it isn't you *must* make the most of it. It'll probably be your last opportunity, ever."

"But I've never been unfaithful to June, Geoff."

"Better late than never. Here she comes."

After Harry had ordered roast kid and Geoff had plumped for lamb chops, Marta put her hand on my shoulder and leant over to point out the steak that she thought I ought to choose. Her face was very close to mine and as she straightened up, her smooth cheek brushed against my stubbly one.

"I'll bring a big salad first, and a plate of octopus, on the house."

"Thanks, Marta. Oh, and could we have a bottle of good red wine, please?"

"Yes, but don't drink too much, Jeremy," she whispered loudly, before sighing and turning to go.

After bringing our food she was busy for a while, but as we ate in silence Geoff's eyes followed her forlornly around the room.

"What a waste," he murmured. "Listen, Jeremy, why don't you get her in the tent, then slip out and I'll pop in and do my stuff?"

"She'd feel your bony body straight away," said Harry with a mouthful of goat meat.

"What's the plan tomorrow then?" I asked.

Geoff glared at Marta's back. "We'll head south. We're behind schedule already."

"We can do three days' driving in two hours, Geoff, on a good road. We've got all the time in the world, but I must say that if a load of scouts are arriving we might be as well to move on. Dessert?"

"More wine first," said Harry.

We decided to skip dessert, as sugar is bad for you, and have wine and cheese instead, which drew a few puzzled glances from the Spaniards, who must not round off their meals in that healthy and civilised fashion. The only problem with our little game was that neither Marta nor I had suggested how we might end it with a flourish, but though she'd been rushed off her feet, she'd found time to pen a little note, which she slid into my shirt pocket when we finally ordered coffee.

"What does it say?" Geoff asked, eyes bulging.

"I'll read it later," I said, before washing down the last of the brie with a slug of wine.

"Oh, come on!"

I extracted the note, read it, smiled, and slipped it back into my pocket.

"Well?"

"Oh, I'd rather not discuss it. I'll take the floor again tonight. I might slip out for a bit later on, but I'll try not to wake you," I said with insouciance.

"Good for you," said Harry, patting his taut belly. "I'd say give her one for me, but I'm not that crude."

"Oh, if I go, I'm sure we'll just chat. Like you said, Geoff, she's probably looking for a father figure and it'd be irresponsible to take advantage of her."

"Fool. I'll give you a condom anyway, as the flesh is weak."

"All right, just in case."

Our ample dinner had made us all sleepy and soon after climbing into his bag, Harry was snoring away. I heard Geoff yawning and fidgeting for a while, no doubt hoping to witness my departure, but I think I just managed to stay awake for longer than him.

Marta's note had said:

Great to meet you, Jeremy.
Stay in touch.
Love, Marta XXX

And she'd written her email address below. Maybe she did fancy me a tiny bit, I thought when I awoke the next morning, before dismissing such Geoff-like nonsense from my mind.

5

As Saturday was Marta's day off, I knew that having coffee and croissants in the restaurant would do nothing to dispel Geoff's uncertainty regarding my nocturnal activities. When a pleasant young chap had served us I yawned loudly and asked who was going to drive.

"I'll go in the back. I feel a bit tired," I added, wiping my bleary eyes, though I'd slept like a log.

"I've looked at the map and there's a really windy road ahead of us, which can only mean a mountain pass," said Geoff, who seemed set on airbrushing my success and his failure from history.

"I hope Bambi's up to it," said Harry.

"I'll nurse her over the hills," Geoff said. "Come on, let's hit the road."

Beyond the village the road narrowed considerably and Geoff had to approach each bend at a snail's pace, allowing us to enjoy the wonderful scenery. The sun popped out from behind the clouds occasionally, and with the windows down the smell of the moistened earth wafted into the cab. I'd discovered that by wedging a camp chair between the benches I could travel like a normal passenger, bar the seatbelt, and I thought it unlikely that a police car would venture down a road which seemed to be exclusively for our own use. We climbed steadily for a while, but when we reached the first hairpin bend, now above the treeline, the gradient increased, but Bambi was equal to it and trundled happily along in second gear. I doubt very much that she'd have made it over some of the torturous passes in the Lake District – like Hardknott and Wrynose, where the tarmac looks like it's been poured down the mountainside – and I was glad that in Spain they appeared to follow the sensible continental custom of zigzagging up hills.

On reaching the summit a sign welcomed us to Castilla y León, and a glance back confirmed that we were leaving Cantabria.

"Pull over there! Let's at least take a last look before we go," I said, disappointed that our sojourn in that province had been so brief.

Geoff steered her onto a little layby and we clambered out. Another sign told us that we were 1316 metres above sea level – a touch lower than Ben Nevis – and until the sun came out a few moments later it was distinctly chilly up there.

"Cantabria's gone quick," said Harry, echoing my thoughts.

"Yes, we're in the province of Burgos now, but that doesn't mean the scenery's going to change," said Geoff. "At the next village we ought to stock up on bread and wine, and camp out in the hills tonight. We don't want to be going to campsites every night."

"Why not?" asked Harry.

"I like campsites," I said.

"Because we've come here for adventure, haven't we?"

"Jeremy's done all right so far," said Harry, making me think that it would soon be time to own up to my celibate night, or Harry would end up taunting Geoff all the way to Gibraltar.

"Hmm, well, we'll press on a bit further into the mountains and find a really wild spot to camp," Geoff said, returning to the van.

In the event the descent of that mountain pass proved to be our last for a while. Rather than heading into another lush valley, when the trees reappeared they were less copious and the meadows less verdant. When the road finally widened to two lanes it felt like we'd arrived in a different country, as though the scenery was still pleasant, it wasn't a patch on what we'd seen in Cantabria, where I rather thought I might return with June one day, but not in Bambi. As for villages, well, the first one we reached was called Espinosa de los Monteros, by far the largest conurbation we'd seen since Liérganes, and about twenty miles from the campsite.

"Is it worth stopping here?" Geoff asked, showing no signs of stopping.

"It's worth stopping practically everywhere," I said. "Let's have a wander round and do a bit of shopping before deciding where to head next."

After buying bread, milk, wine, a few large bottles of water and a roll of clingfilm, Geoff nipped back to the van with them while we waited on a bench in a large square, marred only by a road running right through the middle of it.

"I suppose we'd better look at the churches," Harry said, as we'd already passed a couple.

"We could. Are you interested in that sort of thing?"

"Not really, but that's what you do on holiday, isn't it?" he said with a shrug.

"We'll have a look inside that big one over there and then go for a beer."

"Yes, they're thirsty work those mountain roads."

In the large bar that the three of us soon repaired to, Geoff's eyes followed those of the buxom waitress and after a few minutes' intensive study he declared with relief that she hadn't looked at me once. "Though she did glance at me a couple of times," he added.

"She's more in line with your expectations," said Harry. "She knows she's got no chance with Jeremy and she can probably sense that he's… drained."

I sighed and handed Marta's note to Geoff.

"What does this mean?"

"It means that Marta and I were having you on."

"Ha, I knew it!" His eyes widened with joy and he slapped the table.

"I don't see why you're so chuffed about it," said Harry.

"Oh, I'm not, no, but… well, it just didn't add up. She's probably got a boyfriend and went along with the plan to make sure she didn't weaken and end up in bed with me."

"Yes, I'm sure that was it. Can that be the end of it, please?" I said. "We don't want to spend a month listening to you rabbiting on about women."

"Yes, rather than boring us, keep your thoughts to yourself and impress us with your *actions*," said Harry with an ominous glower, before draining his glass.

"Quite. Not another word, though she just looked over again. Right, let's have a look at the map."

On spreading it out we saw that immediately to the south there were more white patches than green bits.

"How about if we head south to Burgos today? Then we could go south-east into that big green area with lots of picturesque roads and eventually come out at Soria," I said, bearing in mind Frank the cyclist's suggested route and wishing to head stealthily towards the sea. Although I hadn't visited inland Spain I knew there were vast flatlands which I hoped we'd either avoid or whizz through – relatively speaking – on our way to more inspiring terrain.

Harry agreed and Geoff, after a few grunts and a bit of sage nodding, said that we could do worse.

By lunchtime – two o'clock in Spain – we were approaching Burgos after eating up the miles along a straight road through mostly flat, arable land. The road hadn't been very busy, but we'd been pipped at five times, though we were slowly becoming immune to such childish behaviour.

"I believe Burgos is very historic," I said from the back. "But it's not massive, so I think we should park up, have lunch, and take a good look around."

"*That* way," said Harry, pointing firmly ahead, as Geoff appeared to be toying with the idea of making for the bypass. It's strange that Geoff doesn't like large towns and cities, given his appetite for women, who reside there in great numbers, so I told him to chill out as we were well ahead of schedule.

"Where will we sleep tonight?" he asked after parking on a rather rough but free carpark on the outskirts.

"There'll be lots of nice hotels here," said Geoff, winking at me. "I really fancy a jacuzzi, and maybe a massage."

"Ha," was Geoff's response, as he's not so easily taken in.

"The other extreme would be to sleep right here in the carpark," I said. "I bet it'll be empty later on and no-one'll bother us."

With these two contrasting options in mind – though the hotel would have been a huge cop-out – we locked Bambi and strolled into the centre. Burgos is an attractive city with many fine buildings and a huge, traffic-free main square. The vast cathedral dominates the place and we decided to visit it after a quick bite to eat, which was not to include wine and cheese in lieu of dessert. So, after a single beer, a bocadillo and a coffee in the square, we headed that way. Though neither Geoff nor Harry are history buffs or lovers of gothic architecture, even they were impressed by the elaborate edifice, which was begun in 1221, but altered and added to in the fifteenth and sixteenth centuries. We spent a mostly silent half hour inside, admiring the splendid columns and the multitude of ancient sculptures and paintings. Most of the other visitors were tourists too, though unlike them we were far too respectful to take photos, largely because none of us had thought to bring a camera. I snapped the two of them on my old smartphone on the steps outside, before we took a final turn around the building.

"They make you think, places like this, don't they?" said Harry, looking subdued and almost pious.

"What about?" asked Geoff.

"Oh, about how insignificant we are. I'm not one for religion, but in a church like that you get a sense of…"

"Awe?" I chipped in.

"Yes, and a feeling that there might just be someone or something watching over us."

"Hmm, like the bishop's henchmen, who watched over the poor men who slaved away to build it," said Geoff, causing me to sigh and Harry to groan loudly. When he hasn't got women on the brain, another of Geoff's pet subjects is the gross injustice that humankind suffered until socialism appeared on the scene to cure all our ills. Months might pass without him mentioning politics at all, but when he does he comes down squarely in favour of the common man, which, you might think, oughtn't to make us sigh and groan, but, as is often the case with Geoff, he can become decidedly pedantic once he gets started.

The New Labour years were the worst, of course, and I spent many an evening trying to convince him that Tony Blair and company were just as grasping as the Tories, and that as far as I could see they were socialists with an S so small as to be barely visible. When Blair left power and began to dedicate himself to amassing a fortune and buying houses right, left and centre, Harry and I had some fun at Geoff's expense, so politics had lain mostly dormant for quite a while, and the last thing we wanted on our holiday was a recurrence of his left-wing evangelism.

Instead of changing the subject, however, I was stupid enough to suggest that the stonemasons might have earned a decent living.

"Ha, fat chance! No, all this was built upon the exploitation of the common man," he said, theatrically shading his eyes from the shameful structure. "To be honest, I don't think old Jesus would have been too impressed with all these lofty spires and whatnot. He was a revolutionary, after all."

"Religion does give people a lot of comfort though," I said, considering it safer ground. "Especially back then when life was so hard."

"And *why* was life so hard, if the population was low and there was plenty of land for everybody?" he asked, raising his arms in the air and attracting the attention of passing sightseers. "I'll tell you why…"

"Tell someone else," Harry grunted, before heading rapidly towards the nearest bar, with me on his heels. Geoff wandered off in one of his self-righteous huffs.

We sat at a table in the sun, ordered three beers, and began to pore over the map.

It wasn't long before he appeared, after circumnavigating the cathedral again, and slumped down into the vacant chair.

"Just tell me this. If I'm not allowed to talk about women, politics or religion, what the hell *am* I supposed to talk about? It's not my fault that I'm so serious-minded… apart from the women bit."

Harry cleared his throat and sipped his beer. "Jeremy and me have decided that all this has been a mistake," he said, lifting his eyes and gazing at him gravely. "We think it's best if we part company before it's too late and we fall out for good. Bambi's yours, so were going to get our stuff and head off to a hotel for a couple of nights, before going back up north to enjoy the mountains."

"What?"

Although Harry's not exactly cerebral, he can be a damn good actor when an occasion arises that suits his mood. As he'd said nothing to prepare me for this, I could easily understand why Geoff stared at him like a cornered sheep and I felt I had no option but to endorse Harry's opinion, up to a point.

"The thing is, Geoff, that we're only really used to meeting up for a beer now and then. This is proving to be a lot more intense than we expected. I don't mind you talking politics as much as Harry does, but I do think we're a bit incompatible in a situation like this."

"But–"

I raised my hand. "It's you I'm thinking about too, you know. Alone in Bambi you could sow your wild oats right across Spain."

"Like Genghis Khan, without the beard," Harry said.

"But us two oldies are only going to hamper you and cramp your style. I mean, in thirty nights you could have... what? Twenty women?"

"More if he goes to the beach. He could do a double shift down there."

Geoff's still bulging eyes began to narrow and he relaxed his grip on his chair.

"Or start a ticket system, like at the doctors," I said.

"Put an electric screen up on Bambi."

"In a few years Spain'll be full of little Geoffs."

"You pair of bastards! You had me going there, especially considering how well-behaved I've been so far."

I raised my glass. "All for one and one for all."

We clinked glasses and each fell into an amused reverie. Many a true word is spoken in jest, however, and our spell of playacting did give me food for thought. As things stood we'd be spending every hour of the day together. We'd get up together, eat all our meals together, even sleep together – practically – for day after day and I just couldn't see any of us hacking that for a whole month. My thoughts turned to the beach once again. If we could find a nice spot by the sea and set up Harry's tent, we could settle down for maybe a week and each do our own thing to some extent, or at least have the option of doing so.

It's not that I wished to race seaward as fast as Bambi could carry us, but the thought of whiling away the rest of the day in Burgos, probably getting tipsy over dinner again and then sleeping in a carpark, prompted me to suggest making tracks.

"I thought it'd be Geoff who'd say that," said Harry.

"It had crossed my mind," he said. "But I've a feeling that Burgos might be the last city we stay in. What say we stay here tonight, paint the burgh red, and then stick to the countryside from then on?"

"And the beach, a bit," I said.

"Let's vote on it," said Harry. "Who says one last night in civilisation?"

As they both raised their hands, so did I, and I was glad that I'd shaved and showered that morning, as had they. We decided to check on Bambi and while resting assess whether it really would be wise to sleep in the carpark.

"So what you're saying is that instead of sitting down for a slap-up meal, we walk from bar to bar nibbling a bit here and a bit there until we're full," Harry said as we walked back into the centre, slightly more sharply dressed, though not much, and refreshed by a quick wash at the sink.

"Exactly. It's what they do in Spain. Have you never heard of tapas?"

"Nope," he said, though I was sure there were at least a couple of tapas bars in Lancaster. "The trouble is, if I keep walking between bars I'll never get full."

"That's a good point, Harry," I said. "With your metabolism you might end up on a perpetual tapas tour, day and night for the rest of the month."

"Come on, let's stop dawdling. I'm busting for a piss," said Geoff, who had been loath to follow our example of peeing into the large water bottle that Harry had trimmed down with his Swiss Army knife. Wild camping in an urban setting clearly had its drawbacks in a van like Bambi, though we had the portaloo if we really couldn't find anywhere to take a dump. There were still a few cars on the carpark, so we all felt OK about spending the night there.

Geoff employed his slower, standardised Spanish to ascertain where the best tapas bars were, and we made our way towards Calle Sombrerería and found that on the pedestrianised street Saturday night had well and truly begun. All the tables outside the bars were taken, so Geoff led us into one of the least packed establishments where a score or so of youngish people were all talking at the tops of their voices over the Spanish pop music. It had been many years since any of us, except maybe Geoff, had queued three deep at the bar to get a drink, and had he not ushered us into a corner and gone to order, Harry and I would probably have done a runner and gone to find somewhere quieter, with chairs.

"This is typical Burgos blood sausage," Geoff yelled as he plonked a small earthenware bowl onto a narrow ledge and went back to get our beers.

"What do you thi– … hey, it's all gone," he protested on his return.

"There wasn't much of it," Harry mumbled, before patting his mouth with a paper napkin and reaching for his bottle of beer, there being no room for glasses.

Geoff scowled and threaded his way back to the bar, where he ordered several *raciones*, or large tapas, including more Burgos blood sausage, spicy potatoes, boiling prawns, Russian salad, Aranda blood sausage, and some round black discs on bread which also proved to be blood sausage. In the end Harry and I enjoyed a rather stationary tapas tour, while Geoff made repeated trips to the bar for more beer and more tapas, including goat's cheese, which required wine, and so on, until Harry declared that he might just last out until breakfast and why didn't we find somewhere to sit down and have coffee as his legs were aching from standing up.

"*Your* legs are aching," said a slightly sweaty Geoff as we made it outside and breathed in the cool night air. "I felt like a bloody waiter, *and* I paid for the privilege."

"Good man," I said, patting him on the back. "And it took your mind off those gorgeous girls."

"It didn't, but we'll go to a pub later and I'll check out the scene."

Harry and I looked at each other and raised our eyebrows, as neither of us had any intention of re-entering another noisy, crowded place. We soon found a relatively quiet café terrace, with heaters, near the cathedral and settled down to enjoy coffee with a glass of brandy.

"This is more like it," said Harry, easing back in his chair and clasping his hands over his full belly.

"Yes, I like this more too. We can watch the people go by in comfort," I said, relieved to be out of the hectic bar, though the food had been excellent, especially the blood sausage – *morcilla* in Spanish.

"Hmm, don't get too comfortable, because we'll be heading back into the fray in a while, but the pubs don't really get going here till after twelve," Geoff said, his eyes following the passing women, almost all of whom were too young for him. It was a quarter to eleven and Harry and I didn't need to exchange words to agree that there was no way we were going to squeeze our aging bodies into a packed and noisy pub, so we chose to enjoy our time at the café, sipping our brandy and enjoying the buzz of activity around us, but not too near, rather than pointing this out to Geoff and suffering his protests and pleading for an hour.

On finishing his second brandy, Geoff called the waiter. "Right guys, let's hit the pubs and show these youngsters that we're not past it, eh?"

"I'm past it," said Harry.

"Me too. We'll just head back to Bambi, but we'll leave the door unlocked."

"Oh, *come* on. It might be our last night in a city, and a Saturday too."

"That's why we don't want to spoil it," Harry said.

"It's been great, but we're ready for bed. You go ahead and enjoy yourself."

"But don't bring a bird back, as you can't put the tent up on the tarmac," said Harry.

"God, you really are past it."

"Yep, off you go. I'll pay," said Harry, so Geoff strutted off into the night and we ordered another brandy.

"I'll sleep after this," I said half an hour later, feeling tipsy and tired.

"Me too. Come on, let's get back."

As we neared the carpark we both sensed that something wasn't quite right. Despite being a quiet spot near to some warehouses, we both heard a strange thudding noise that proved to be the modern techno music that I can't abide.

"Probably just a car going past," said Harry when he heard it. (Harry hadn't ceased to be rather deaf, by the way, but I've refrained from mentioning the fact repeatedly so as not to bore you.)

"Sounds like it's parked somewhere. I hope they drive off soon, bloody racket."

When we turned the final corner we saw to our horror that Bambi was surrounded by cars and young people, all drinking from large plastic glasses and dancing or bobbing their heads to the execrable boom, boom, boom that emanated from the tailgate of a souped-up Ford Fiesta. There were about thirty of them and none paid any attention to us as we stood on the pavement looking on.

"If there were half as many, I'd drive them off, but I don't think I can handle that lot," said Harry, rocking to and fro on his heels like a policeman in an Ealing comedy.

"They look friendly enough – just normal kids, really – but we're not going to get much sleep."

"I thought I might be getting a bit hard of hearing, but I'm not too sure now. What do we do?"

"If Geoff was here we could just drive off and park somewhere else."

"Maybe he *knew* this was going to happen," he said with a scowl. "How long do you think they'll stay?"

"A long time. They party all night in Spain, I believe. Let's move her across the street over there at least."

As we approached Bambi, who hadn't been molested, a young chap detached himself from his group of boppers and greeted us in fairly fluent English.

"Is that your crazy van, man?" said the thin, black-clad youth with short hair. His eyes looked rather glazed under the dim street lights and I suspected that the dark liquid in his glass wasn't the only mind-altering substance he'd been taking.

"Yes," I said.

"Cool. I saw the English number plate and thought you might be old hippies."

"We're old, but not hippies," Harry said.

"We were going to sleep here," I said.

"What? So early?" he said with a giggle. "Come and have a drink first," he added, taking Harry by the arm and leading him towards the refreshment vehicle, a black, wide-wheeled Seat Ibiza. I cringed as the boy's hand made contact, but Harry is never averse to one more drink and had clearly decided to make the best of it.

Plastic glasses of a cloudy brew were thrust into our hands and a few more people wandered over.

"What's this?" I asked our host.

"Calimocho, man. It's red wine and coke, with a bit of rum."

"It tastes good," I yelled above the music.

Harry sampled his like a wine taster, before downing half of it. "Why do you come here?" he asked the lad.

"Oh, the pubs are too expensive. Many of us have no jobs right now, so what can we do?"

"What?" Harry asked, wiggling his ear.

"Hey, turn that shit down," the boy bellowed in English, and the racket was reduced by about a third.

"You speak good English," I said.

"Been working in London, at a café near Covent Garden, with my mate over there." He pointed to the DJ. "Paco, come over here."

Paco, also dressed in black, was a chunky youth with a mop of wavy hair. After grinning and shaking both our hands in a strangely masonic way he pointed at Bambi.

"Where did you get that beast?"

"What?" said Harry.

"It's our friend's. He's out in the pubs, but we came back early."

"What, *three* of you sleep in that?"

"We try."

The first youth, Jorge by name, took the hint. "I guess you don't like this music much, huh?"

"I'm not too fond of it, no."

"No worries," said Paco, before loping over to the car.

It was a strange, almost surreal experience to hear the strains of Strangers in the Night after the infernal din that had preceded it. I thought the others would protest, but they merely adjusted their dance steps or head bobbing and carried on nattering to each other as if nothing had happened.

"Is that better?" Jorge asked.

"Yes. We're not so old, but yes, it's easier to talk now, thanks."

"The cops'll be round soon, so it was time to turn it down anyway," he said, before asking us where we were heading.

So we chatted with Paco, Jorge and one or two of the others while we sipped our calimocho and the cool night air kept us from feeling sleepy. The police did indeed arrive, about an hour later, but the two cops just stood looking on for a while, the older one tapping his foot to Frank Sinatra's greatest hits. They seemed puzzled by the sedate scene, but their reaction was nothing compared to Geoff's when he approached us, weaving slightly, with his mouth wide open in astonishment. I introduced him to our new friends and Jorge managed to eke out one last calimocho, which Geoff sipped politely, before handing it to Harry.

It was after three by that time and Paco told us that some of them were heading off to a disco.

"You guys wanna come?"

"No thanks, Paco," I said. "It's been great to meet you, but I think we'll turn in now."

"Jeremy and me like to hang out with the young 'uns, you see, Geoff," Harry murmured from his bed. "You know, keep our pulse on the finger of… whatever."

"You're pissed, now go to sleep," he replied from the floor.

"How was your evening, Geoff?" I asked.

"Oh, all right. An old bag pestered me in one pub, but I managed to shake her off."

"How old was she?"

"Oh, well over forty. By far the oldest woman in the place. Why she picked on me I just don't know."

6

It was about ten when I peeped through the shabby little curtain the following morning, having woken due to the sun having turned Bambi into a sauna. Being a Sunday, there were few cars on the carpark and when I'd edged past a sleeping Geoff and clambered out I was surprised to see very little litter from the night before, as I didn't remember them clearing it up. It wasn't too hot outside – maybe twenty degrees – but I feared that Bambi would become a veritable inferno in really hot weather. When I grabbed a bottle of water from the fridge I saw all the perishable food that we hadn't eaten and decided it was time for us to take a walk, or drive, on the wild side and get back to basics for a few days, as I'd already done more drinking than was good for me and we'd eaten practically every meal out.

When Harry emerged I nipped back inside to retrieve the camping chairs from over the cab and we sat in the shade, passing the water bottle to and fro.

"How do you feel?" he asked.

"Not too bad. That calimocho stuff can't have been too noxious and I guess we didn't drink that much of it."

"I did." He rubbed his temples and yawned.

"I was just thinking that we ought to get back into the countryside for a few days and start fending for ourselves a bit more."

"Me too. My diet and exercise regime hasn't exactly got off to a good start."

"No."

"I need to take a dump."

"Me too, but not with Geoff there on the floor. He's bound to wake up."

"He'll probably analyse our shit."

"Ugh, please, Harry! Let's get him up and go off to find a bar."

"I'll go and give him a gentle prod."

A yelp soon followed and before long we'd packed away our bedding, put away the chairs, and headed off in the most promising direction. A few blocks away we found a scruffy bar and quickly ordered coffee and toast.

"Who's going first?" I asked.

"I'm busting," said Harry, so off he went.

"What's the bog like?" Geoff asked when he came back looking relieved.

"It was all right till I went in there. No window, I'm afraid."

Geoff's expression when he returned was of mingled relief and nausea, so I sipped my coffee and toughed it out for a few more minutes, but it still wasn't pleasant and the portly owner and a couple of customers up at the bar looked at me oddly on my return.

"It's got to be a campsite tonight," said Harry, and even Geoff didn't argue with that, maybe because he had the worse hangover of all, caused, he claimed, by the bad whisky in the pubs.

"The sods charge you six euros and then give you garrafón, the thieves," he said, swilling the coffee around in his mouth.

"What's that? I asked.

"Cheap spirits that they put in the bottles. If I ever got a hangover back in my Jaén days, it was because of garrafón."

"Never because you drank too much?" Harry asked.

"No, I might not be… oversized like you, but I can hold my whisky. Shame it's too dear in England, or I'd have drunk you under the table more than once."

Although he wasn't talking about women, politics or religion, I still wished to change the subject.

"So, today's plan." I slapped the map before opening it. "I suggest we head south-east and find a campsite somewhere in these green and pleasant hills."

"And we stay away from bars," said Harry.

"And eat up our food," said Geoff.

"And do some walking," I added, glad that we were in agreement.

Harry suggested that we buy a couple of knapsacks and waterproof jackets, but Geoff pointed out that shops didn't open on Sundays in Spain.

"They still respect the worker a bit more than we do. If our man here sells us some bread, we'll make a do," he said, before rising and approaching the bar.

Funnily enough the owner spoke much more than Geoff on this occasion and when he returned with two baguettes he was keen to leave.

"Something up?" I asked.

"Nope," he said, before surprising us both by extracting a twenty euro note from his wallet, holding it up to the light, and slapping it harshly onto the table, before stomping out.

"Gracias," said the owner, before pointing out his windfall to his cronies and cackling like a baritone witch.

Geoff then told us that on asking the man for a couple of *barras* of bread, the oaf had launched into an ironic diatribe about us using his bar as a hotel and takeaway, before asking him if he wouldn't like to pop upstairs for a bath while he was at it, as his wife would be more than willing to scrub his back.

"Ha, that's quite funny," said Harry.

"Yes, but it was the *way* he said it. Some of these Castilians can be so... uppity. Folk are more down to earth in Andalucia."

"In Jaén, you mean, as you know the rest of it about as well as we do," said Harry.

"Bah!"

"The chap had a point though, but he's done all right out of it," I said, suppressing a chuckle.

"Yes, it cost me, but there's no doubt who won *that* little dispute. Come on, let's get out of this damn city."

About ten miles to the east of Burgos we found ourselves on an excellent minor road heading back into green, undulating countryside. After passing a large reservoir I indicated a right-hand turn and Geoff steered us southwards past another reservoir and into wilder terrain. The road became sinuous for a while and I realised that looking at the map was making me feel queasy, so I desisted.

"How are you doing back there?" I asked a so far silent Harry.

"Middling. Are we nearly there yet?" he asked from his central position which seemed to aid Bambi's stability.

"I don't know where we're going." I risked another peek at the map and saw a place that I liked the sound of. "We'll head towards Quintanar de la Sierra, I reckon, unless we see a decent-looking campsite before then. What do you think, Geoff?"

"I don't. I'm on autopilot right now. Bloody garrafón."

As often happens in Spain, the road then narrowed for no apparent reason, so when we reached a village called Barbadillo del Pez (Little Beard of the Fish?) I saw no reason not to take an equally narrow road to the east, which took us through some really stunning scenery. During the last twenty miles of our journey we saw only two or three cars and I felt I'd made a fortuitous choice when we saw a sign to a campsite just as we entered Quintanar, a biggish village, scruffy a first sight, but which got slightly better as we chugged into the centre, though it was clearly no tourist mecca.

Geoff pulled over near the plaza mayor, boasting a small but stately town hall and a couple of other fine buildings, but which also offered great views over the surrounding countryside. We had driven about seventy miles on mostly narrow roads practically non-stop and were all keen to stretch our legs.

"Thanks for driving all that way, Geoff," I said.

"No problem. It took my mind off my stomach. Bambi's really quite nice to drive when you get used to her," he said, looking at Harry, who was yet to take the wheel.

"I'll take your word for it. Ooh, look over there. Hostal – Bar Casa Ramon. Food and beds both conveniently situated under one roof. I bet it's cheap too."

"We'll have a drink, but we're going to the campsite and we're going to eat our food," I said, leading the way over to the modern four-storey stone building opposite the town hall.

When the waiter came we all found ourselves ordering beer – due, Harry claimed, to us always drinking beer whenever we met up – and when he asked us if we were going to have lunch Geoff felt that the least we could do was sample their tapas, so we did, about a dozen of them, plus two more beers each.

"I suppose we'd better have coffee now," said Geoff.

"It'd be rude not to," said Harry.

"Yes, and *then* we're going to the campsite," I said. "Though I must say I feel better for that."

Camping Arlanza is about a mile from Quintanar, situated on a large, flat piece of land dotted with oak, beech and pine trees. A river runs down the west side of the site and, as if that weren't enough, there are also two swimming pools, one of them huge, the use of both being included in the very modest price. It must be an absolute mecca for families in summer, but when we arrived it wasn't busy at all – just a handful of tents and four full-scale camper vans. The helpful chap in reception showed us to a large plot not far from the river, before telling us that the restaurant was open all day, every day.

"Excellent," said Harry, patting his paunch.

"No, no. You've only just eaten and we've got loads of stuff we've got to finish off." I looked up at the sky and judged the few clouds to be benign ones. "Shall we put the tent up?"

"I'll put it up, as it's mine, and I'm going to sleep in it," said Harry, before scuttling into the van to get it.

Geoff and I settled ourselves in our camp chairs and watched Harry cut the plastic from the brand-new tent with the scissors of his ubiquitous Swiss Army knife, though it'd have been easier to tear it open.

"It's a dome tent," Geoff murmured. "They can be tricky to put up, especially the first time."

"Shall we help?"

"Nah. Look, he's already got the colour coding wrong with the poles."

"Harr–"

"Shush, he wants to do it himself. I bet it's the first tent he's put up for forty years."

"More. He left the scouts at fifteen, under a cloud," I said, just loud enough for our already sweating friend to hear me.

"Not for anything dodgy… just smoking," he grunted.

"That's what I meant, a cloud of smoke. I didn't know you were colour-blind, Harry."

"Eh?"

"The pole with yellow bits goes in the yellow slots."

"Oh, shit." He pulled it out, or tried to, as the elastic stretched and split the pole, leaving him pulling one piece of it while the rest remained in the narrow sleeve.

When the elastic reached an alarming length, I suggested slotting the sections back together and pushing the pole out.

"I was going to say that, but I thought he'd work it out for himself eventually. Trial and error, that's the best way to learn," said Geoff, smiling placidly.

By the time Harry had pushed the pole through the tight fabric slots, the clouds had dispersed and the sweat had begun to roll off him. He finally got the first and easiest of the three poles in place, before slotting another together and ramming it into its sleeve.

"This is going in easier," he panted as he fed the pole through the first sheath and missed the second.

"You'll have to start again, I'm afraid," Geoff said in a doom-laden voice. "Look, it's waggling in the air."

"It'd be easier with two," I said in a conciliatory tone, becoming worried by the colour of Harry's face. It wasn't a heart attack I feared, however, but an outbreak of wrath, like the time a gangly student had pinched his chair in a pub in Lancaster while he was at the bar. That time he'd just grasped the skinny youth under the arms, lifted him high in the air, told him he hated bloody students, and deposited him on the floor, but as a few children had sidled up to view the tent-erecting spectacle, I feared that Geoff might soon end up in the river if he continued to goad him.

"It's *his* tent, and *he's* going to put it up," said Geoff, oblivious.

After drying his brow on his t-shirt, Harry finally shoved the pole through all the sheaths and stood viewing the taut, half-erected shelter.

"Does it really need the third pole?" he asked.

"Oh, yes, indeed it does," said Geoff, pulling faces for the kids and pointing at Harry's broad back.

The last pole is always the hardest, and though those tents are strongly constructed, I doubted the green fabric would withstand the tremendous thrusts that Harry subjected it to as he rammed it mercilessly from sheath to sheath as the structure billowed this way and that as if it had a life of its own.

Finally one of the children, a boy of about eleven, came to Harry's aid and held the recalcitrant sheath in position while the grunting ogre slid it into place.

"Despacio," said the boy, meaning slowly, and after another two minutes of patient effort the lad hooked the pole into its ring.

The tent fell gently to earth in the shape its makers had intended, while Harry dropped to the ground like a stone, or boulder, and flopped back on the grass. By the time he sat up, the lad and his two companions – a boy and a girl slightly younger than him – had slid the inner tent from the bag and were busily hooking it into place. The girl then smiled benignly at Harry and said something unintelligible.

"She's asking you which way round you want it," Geoff said. "Do you want it facing Bambi, the river, Mecca, or what?"

His anger quelled by the presence of his juvenile assistants, Harry pushed himself to his feet and indicated that he would like the doorway facing directly away from our van.

"Because I don't want to look at those two silly men," he said, pointing at us.

"Silly men not help," she replied, shaking her finger at us, which I thought a bit harsh, as I'd been more than willing to lend a hand.

Harry then helped his helpers to bang in the pegs and attach the guy ropes, before pronouncing the word 'ice-cream' very slowly and licking his fist.

"They all study English at school," said Geoff.

"Yes, please," said the children, so Harry avoided further embarrassment by grabbing his wallet and allowing himself to be led to the campsite restaurant by his entourage.

Geoff suggested repositioning the inner tent so that he wouldn't be able to get through the door.

"I don't think so, Geoff. Let's have a bit of peace and harmony in these harmonious surroundings."

"Yes, at least we won't have to listen to his snoring tonight."

"Hmm, and maybe for a couple more nights. We could do worse than stay here for a while, you know."

He looked up at the pristine sky. "We'll get behind schedule."

"Nonsense. After here we could nip down to Soria and then head south towards Cuenca," I said, having become quite familiar with the northern half of my Michelin map collection. "Cuenca's about half way there, and it's only... six days since we left Lancaster."

"Is that all?"

"Yes, Bambi's blazing a trail. Mind you, we'll lengthen the route by heading down to the coast, maybe south of Murcia, but we've got loads of time," I said nonchalantly.

"The coast?" he said, screwing up his nose.

"Yes, but not to any big tourist places. Just imagine waking up right on the seafront and going for a swim before breakfast."

He grunted.

"It'll be much warmer down there too."

"But mucked up with foreigners."

"Well, there might be a few intrepid camper-vanners like us around."

"Yes, tight-wad Dutch geriatrics still eating their mouldy Edam cheese."

I thought he was probably right, so I tried a different tack. "The campsites will be more cosmopolitan down there by the sea. Lots of healthy young people, I imagine, from all over Europe. Footloose, fancy-free and looking for a good time. Quite a few Scandinavians, I imagine."

"Hmm, did I ever tell you about Freya?"

"Er, you might have mentioned her," I said, before he launched into an account of his steamy summer with the sultry Swedish chambermaid for the umpteenth time. Neither Harry nor I ever saw Freya – not even a photo – but from Geoff's description, Ingrid Bergmann and Greta Garbo would have paled beside her incomparable charm and beauty, which made us wonder why she'd been making beds at a second-rate hotel in Ambleside.

"… and then she vanished into thin air," he concluded, once again.

"Shame, but there are more Nordic fish in the sea. I suggest we stay here for three or four nights and explore the area. There are bound to be things to see, and we can do some great walks."

Geoff looked up and shaded his eyes. "Yes, and get a really good tan before we hit the beach."

"I wonder where Harry's got to?" I asked, feeling that I'd said enough for the time being. Over the following days Geoff would assimilate my proposed route and by the time we set off it would have been his idea all along.

"Shall we go and see?"

"Yes, let's see what he's up to."

It transpired that after treating the kids and himself to huge ice creams, they had wandered over to their tents – two large family ones – and our friend was speaking fluently to the two sets of parents. Speaking fluent English, that is, as we heard a stocky, distinguished-looking Spaniard quizzing him about his life back home, while the other three adults chipped in when they could, all looking delighted to have the massive Englishman in their midst. The kids, finding their new friend and benefactor usurped, had wandered off towards the river, still licking and munching away.

"Shall we go and introduce ourselves?" I asked.

Geoff put his hand on my arm. "Good god, no! Can't you see what they're doing?"

"Er, talking?"

"They've latched onto the great lump like limpets so they can practise their English on him. Look at the short woman with a face like a stevedore. Look at her bulging eyes and rapt expression. She's lapping it up and just waiting to get a word in," he said from our refuge beside a tree.

We observed in silence for a while and what Geoff asserted appeared to be true. Though we both find Harry moderately entertaining, that's because he's an old friend with a certain way about him, but to look at the four of them you'd have thought he'd just stepped out of the jungle after discovering a lost city. They hung on his every word and when he'd filled them in about one mundane matter, another badly pronounced question would lead him onto new ground. I don't remember exactly how the conversation went, but this is a snippet from memory:

"… and next to Lancaster is Morecambe, a sea-side town where many bad people live."

"Bad people. How they bad?"

"Oh, people with no jobs, alcoholics, students, you know."

"Students they bad? They not study?"

"Some, I suppose, but they wear stupid clothes and make the locals angry, so they have to beat them up."

"What is beat up, please?"

"Er, thump," he said, thumping the palm of his hand. "So this very bad for my job," he added, simplifying his grammar for their benefit.

"You policeman for long time?"

"Yes, I started in nineteen…"

And so they went on, making me glad that Geoff had arrested my forward motion, or all three of us would have been facing an inquisition which promised to be interminable. We sloped off to the river, followed its burbling course for a while, and strolled back to our pitch.

When we returned from our shaves and showers a while later, Harry had extracted his holdall and was rooting through his clothes. He looked up and smiled briefly, before selecting a soft but crinkled blue shirt and holding it up to the fading light.

"Going somewhere?" Geoff asked him.

"Oh, Juan, Paula and… the others have invited me to a barbeque. It seemed rude to refuse."

Geoff nudged me. "What time do they want us there?"

"Oh, er, it's just me they've invited. I mentioned you, I think, but I didn't like to presume. They might not have enough food for all of us."

"That's all right, Harry. Me and Jeremy can eat up the stale bread and rancid cheese."

"There are plenty of tins, under the left-hand bench. Sorry, lads, but that's just the way it's worked out."

"What do they do?" I asked.

"What do who do?"

"Your new friends. What jobs do they do? They look quite well-to-do, so I thought they might have interesting jobs."

"Hmm, to be honest, I'm not sure. I think Juan said he was a lawyer or something, but they seemed more interested in me."

At this point I thought Geoff's satirical side might come into play, and after leading Harry on he'd unsubtly point out that they just wanted to practise their English on him, but he did no such thing, instead saying that he felt like a quiet night anyway.

"Me too. You go and socialise for a bit while we chill out here. It's good for us to do our own thing from time to time anyway," I said, half wishing that Geoff was joining him so that I could read quietly for a while, but neither of the women warranted his attentions.

In the event I did read, as after our dinner of ravioli on bread, Geoff picked up his latest fantasy novel – just the genre for him – and we whiled away a pleasant couple of hours until Harry's return at about eleven.

As he approached our rapidly dimming lantern my first impression was that he'd been hitting the bottle again, as his gait was ponderous and his head bowed. He slumped down into the vacant chair and exhaled with a long, resounding sigh.

"Good dinner?" I asked.

"Yes, good food. Chops, ribs… all good," he said wearily.

"You look done in," said Geoff.

"My head's spinning. I've never talked so much or been asked so many questions in my life. I couldn't even get a sausage down me before someone asked another question. I never thought I was that interesting."

"The Spaniards are a naturally curious race," Geoff said. "Did any of them speak much?"

"They tried, they really tried, but their English is pretty crap, so they just asked another question, then when I answered asked me to say it again. In the end I was talking like Pocahontas so they'd get what I was saying."

"Well, you got some nice grub and met some real natives. We've just been reading," I said. "Oh, and we've been looking at the map and think we'll drive back up the road tomorrow and take a walk to see some lakes up in the hills."

"Me too."

"Of course."

"No, I mean I'm going to some lakes too, with them."

"With your new pals?" Geoff asked with glee.

"I liked the idea at first, early on, then I couldn't get out of it. We're going in both their cars. I hope I get a couple of the kids in mine. At least they just chat like normal human beings."

"Ha, an excellent plan!" Geoff said, before hooting with laughter. "So, your former best friends will follow your new best friends in Bambi and we *might* meet up somewhere along the way."

"Though it's a large area," I said.

"With several lakes," said Geoff.

"*Please* try to meet us. If you don't I'll end up throttling one of them."

7

After further pleas over breakfast the next morning we agreed to jump into Bambi the moment they drove away and follow them up the mountain. Geoff had poo-pooed Harry's offer of a formal introduction as, he'd insisted, neither of us wished to share a picnic lunch with a party of linguistic and cultural vultures.

"No, we'll just follow you. If we can't keep up, tell them to slow down a bit," I said. "We'll park nearby and maybe meet you later on."

"Can I call you if I get really desperate?"

"*All* right then," said Geoff, patting his huge but sagging shoulder. "But you've got yourself into this and you must only call as a last resort. Jeremy and I wish to savour the scenery in silence. I doubt we'll exchange more than a handful of words all day. Off you go now. That female Marty Feldman is waving at you."

The absence of Harry and some of our gear lightened Bambi's load considerably and I was able to follow their Volvo and BMW up into the hills without difficulty, as they negotiated the bends with great caution.

"Harry's up front in the BMW," Geoff said. "He must be mesmerising the driver, as in a machine like that I'd be up at the lakes already."

After a few miles we turned left onto a single-track road which led us through forests of tall pines, and Bambi chugged happily along behind the powerful cars. Although she looked pretty naff, I had to admit that she punched above her weight and I began to realise that the engine which powered so many millions of utility vehicles – mainly in the Third World – was a really robust, efficient one. When we reached a large, almost empty carpark, Harry's chums carried on up the road, but Geoff suggested that we park up and walk from there, as if we pulled up alongside them we might get roped into the verbal quagmire.

As we still lacked knapsacks, I'd emptied my large rucksack in order to carry our sandwiches, water and spare clothes in a dignified manner, as both of us had agreed that with plastic bags over our shoulders we'd bring disgrace on our nation. Harry had been firmly instructed to carry no food, as a sumptuous picnic lunch was to be provided by his hosts, so at least he had that to look forward to.

We set off along the well-signposted path and headed up through the forest in the cool morning air. The sun soon warmed us as we strode briskly up the slope and I reminded Geoff to make use of the sun cream that I'd already applied to my face and limbs.

"Nah, I need to get a tan if we're going to the coast. The birds'll expect it. Besides, it's not that warm."

"It might be deceptive."

"I'm used to it. I got as brown as the peasants down in Jaén."

"That was a long time ago."

"The human body doesn't forget."

"OK, you know where it is… if you want it," I panted, as he was settling a blistering pace, but I was determined to keep up.

After less than an hour the first of the Lagunas de Neila came into view. They were tarns rather than lakes, especially the first two small ones we saw, nestled in their tree-lined hollows and as clear as glass. The surrounding 2000 metre peaks were splendid and there wasn't a soul around. After taking a few photos we headed west to the larger and more exposed tarns. The few walkers we saw there – some of them inappropriately shod – all arrived on a path from the north, so we headed that way and soon saw a large, incongruous building down below; incongruous due to the fact that it oughtn't to have been there at all; a bothy maybe, but not that two-storey stone structure surrounded by smaller buildings so high up in the mountains. In the Lake District it wouldn't be allowed, of course, but I guess if that's what it takes to get people into the wilderness, so be it.

"It looks like a hotel or restaurant," Geoff said, peering down with disapproval.

"Or both. I think I can make out their cars down there."

"You have eyes like a hawk, Jeremy. Can you spot a giant surrounded by jabbering Spaniards?"

"No, but I don't want to get any closer to find out. Let's go back to the tarn and have our lunch."

After scoffing our butties and applying or not applying more sun cream, we rested for a while before heading down to see how fate had treated our friend. We'd expected to see them appear on the path to take a peek at the nearest tarn, but they'd either climbed up another way or stayed put at the picnic site which we discerned as we descended the path. It was tempting to skirt by and head down the road to find Bambi, but we'd promised Harry that we'd put in an appearance so we strolled towards the benches and picnic tables, nipping from tree to tree in order to eavesdrop if we could.

"… and beef and pork. Yes, we eat all the same meat in England," were the first words we heard.

"You want some more?" the less ugly of the wives asked him.

"No, thanks. I'm completely stuffed."

"Stuffed? What is stuffed, Harry?"

"Full, very full."

"More wine, Harry?" asked the man called Juan.

"Go on then."

"What mean go on then?" asked Señora Feldman.

"*Yes*, it means yes," his rather strained and slightly slurred voice said as he held up his glass.

"I'd hoped it'd be coffee time by now," Geoff murmured.

"I think it is for the others. It's just Harry who's sticking to the wine. He can get stroppy when he's drunk."

"Don't I know it? Come on, let's play the knights in shining armour," he said, which I thought apt, as his skin was looking pretty shiny by that stage; shiny and red.

"Thank f*ck you've come," Harry muttered as we approached the table. Despite being seated in the shade of the trees, he was almost as red and shiny as Geoff and beads of sweat were trickling down his temples. The children had abandoned him to his fate and were playing some way off. "*These*," he almost shouted, "are my friends. Geoff, Jeremy, *please* meet Juan, Paula, Federico and Lourdes."

Geoff introduced himself in Spanish, but this aberration was politely ignored and they responded in execrable English. Our hands were shaken, even by the women, who perhaps thought it was more English to dispense with the usual two kisses.

"You want some coffee?" asked Lourdes (Marty). "We finish eat, but Harry he very hunger and thirsting."

"Above all thirsty. Yes, a coffee would be great, thank you," I said.

She duly dispensed the thick black liquid into two small plastic cups, before offering us some dainty little cakes.

"Delicious," I said after taking a bite.

"I make them."

"Where are you from?" asked Geoff.

"From Madrid. And where is you–"

"What do you do, Lourdes?" he interrupted.

"What I do?"

"Yes, what jobs do you all do?"

"Er, my husband and Juan they lawyers."

"Very interesting." Geoff turned to the men. "Do you think the Spanish economy is now improving?" He looked from one to the other with fanatically friendly eyes.

"I think so, yes. Slowly it get better," said Federico, a short, scrawny chap who I think Geoff had judged less likely to retaliate with questions of his own.

"How long are you staying at the campsite?" I asked, keen to reinforce Geoff's diversionary strategy, as Harry had now put down his glass and was looking on with gratitude in his bleary eyes.

"We leave tomorrow," said Paula, keen to get a word in.

"Have you enjoyed yourselves?"

"Yes, it good…"

This quick-fire interrogation went on for a while longer, before Geoff put down his empty cup, slapped his thighs, stood up, and stretched out his hand.

"It's been an indescribably rousing and gratifying experience to come across such a scintillating throng of devotees of the great outdoors in this sun-spangled utopia of verdant hummocks," he said at great speed, before beginning to pump hands. "Verily Jeremy and I are elated to have been privileged to sup this goblet of brown kindness with thee, but we must wend our weary way down the mountainside and jabber not a moment longer. Good afternoon and thank you. Chin up, Harry. Come on Jeremy," he concluded, before guiding me through the trees and onto the road.

I glanced back once and saw that conversation had yet to be resumed. I hoped they wouldn't ask Harry to decipher Geoff's ludicrous rant, but I rather thought they'd overlook it.

"Was that the right thing to do?" I asked Geoff as we loped along towards the lower carpark.

"Well, it saved us from their clutches and I think it's taken the wind out of their sails a bit. Despite their free classes with Harry they'll have realised that they know bugger all English, so they might leave him in peace."

"I hope so. He was looking rough, and tetchy, and if we'd been nicer we might have found ourselves invited to a farewell dinner tonight. I'm glad they're off tomorrow."

"Me too. That would never have happened back in my Jaén days. I think I liked the Spaniards more before they got this burning desire to learn English. I hope I don't see that lot again."

As things turned out, an hour later we were extremely glad to see them again. On spying Bambi through the trees I noticed something odd about her, and on drawing closer we saw that her left-hand rear tyre was flat.

"Damn it," I said.

"We'll soon have her jacked up and change the wheel. I can do it in less than five minutes."

"Have we got one of those sealant sprays? If it's a slow puncture we could use that."

Geoff tutted and shook his head. "Short-term solution, Jeremy, as we'd never be sure about the tyre. No, I'll pop the spare on and we can get the puncture fixed tomorrow. There's bound to be some sort of garage in a village that size."

"I guess so," I said, pleased that it would buy me at least another day in that delightful place.

Geoff unlocked the door and leapt inside. "Here's the jack. Make a start while I dig out the spare."

I positioned and tightened the jack, but decided to wait for Geoff to alight with the wheel before loosening the bolts and lifting the van. A couple of minutes later his crimson face appeared around the door.

"Er, one small problem, Jeremy."

"Don't tell me the spare's flat."

"No, it isn't flat."

"Bald?"

"Nope."

"Absent?"

"Yep, afraid so. I must have been too busy checking everything else to ask about the spare." He scratched his head and smiled, looking a bit like Stan Laurel after a minor explosion, so sunburnt was his face.

"Shame that very nice man who sold it you didn't tell you."

"He probably forgot too. Oh well, it'll have to be the spray after all." He waggled the rusty can in the air as if not having checked the spare wheel was a minor matter, but Geoff has never been one for owning up to his mistakes.

Unfortunately the spray didn't work, having probably spent the last decade in the damp cupboard under the sink. We looked at each other and frowned, reading each other's thoughts. There had been about twenty vehicles up by the hotel and most were yet to descend. We were sure to be able to beg or buy a can of spray from one car or another, but knew we were fated to wait for the people Geoff had just bamboozled with his facetious little speech.

"I'll do the talking," I said.

"I'll wait in Bambi."

"No you bloody won't, though you could do with getting out of the sun for a bit."

Geoff looked down at his rosy arms and legs. "Just wait till tomorrow. I always go brown overnight."

"I hope so, for your sake. Here they come." I dashed to the roadside and flagged down the Volvo, before explaining my predicament to Juan.

"Hmm, my wheels not go down, or when go down I still drive. Special wheels. I think Federico he have spray. I go ask."

"Thanks, Juan," I said humbly.

Federico, as well as having three sleeping children in the back of his car – Harry and the two boys – also had a can of sealant which he proceeded to spray into Bambi's deflated tyre. I held my breath, and so did the tyre, as a crouching Geoff proclaimed the repair a success.

"Thank you very much, Federico," he said, slowly and clearly. "Tomorrow we will buy another can of spray and give it to you."

"No necessary, and tomorrow we go soon. Now you go first so we see you OK."

"Thank you," Geoff said with a contrite little bow.

"Splendid folk the Spaniards, really," he said as he cautiously piloted Bambi down into the valley.

"Maybe we should invite them all to dinner at the restaurant," I said, as we could hardly offer them tinned curry or steak in gravy.

"Do we have to?"

"I think so. I'll do it."

When we returned safe and sound I did so, and they accepted, on one condition, that they pay for the meal.

"No, no, I *insist* on paying," I said, patting my chest.

"No, look, Jeremee, you men… this old van… better we pay then you have money to go home," Juan said with a compassionate smile.

I laughed and raised my hands, probably a bit like Rigsby in Rising Damp when trying to impress Miss Jones. "No, Juan, I was a teacher, Harry a policeman, and Geoff… a lot of things. We have money. Bambi, the van, is like a joke for us," I said, laughing again to prove it.

Juan grasped my shoulder and moved it to and fro. "Jeremee, but now you retire. Listen, Federico and me, we lawyers. Crisis in Spain very good for we. Lot of company go caput, we make much money. *We* pay tonight."

"All right then, if you insist."

"Nine o'clock, yes?"

"Yes, gracias."

"De nada," he said, which proved not to be his last words in Spanish, as during the dinner Geoff managed to string together enough phrases to convince them that he really could speak it, so while Juan, Federico and Geoff chatted mostly in Spanish, and Harry sat down at the end of the table with the kids, I bore the brunt of Paula and Lourdes's undiminished anglophilia. By the end of the meal I'd told them my life story, in very simple terms, and though I'd found it tiresome I was pleased that my two mates were able to enjoy themselves, but I decided that they owed me one.

They repaid my selflessness by sorting Bambi out the next morning – a new tyre and a second-hand spare wheel which the garage owner assured them would fit – while I walked along the river and enjoyed my solitude. Geoff had slept badly and noisily, due to his burning skin, but even the fact that his nose had begun to peel didn't convince him that a golden tan was not to be the result of his reckless exposure.

"I see you've bought some after-sun cream though," I said on their return.

"Yes, it'll help to consolidate my tan. By the time we reach the beach I'll be a veritable Adonis, irresistible to all the northern belles."

"You look like a fried tomato," said Harry.

"You'll see. I'm awash with melanin. It's pumping through my veins as we speak."

Unsure that melanin worked quite like that, I broached the subject of our onward journey. "You sound a bit keener on the beach now, Geoff. Shall we put some miles in tomorrow and maybe get as far as Cuenca?"

"Ah, Cuenca! The hanging houses! The... gorge, I think. Yes, let's toddle off down there tomorrow."

"Is that all right with you, Harry?"

"Eh? Oh, I don't mind where we go, though I'd like to see the sea within a few days."

Later on I took a sneaky look at google maps on my phone and saw that the recommended route to Cuenca would take about four hours in a normal vehicle, so Bambi would need at least five. Forewarned is forearmed, so on reaching Alcolea del Pinar at noon the next day – about a hundred miles to the south – I vetoed Geoff's suggestion that we head straight for Cuenca along the torturous-looking mountain roads.

"No, Geoff, the main road's going to be hard enough work by the look of things, and we've still got over a hundred miles to go."

"Main road," said Harry from the back.

"Do you fancy driving for a bit?"

"No."

"You haven't had a go yet," said Geoff. "Jeremy's done the first stretch and I'm feeling a bit itchy – must be that damn cream – so I think it's your turn."

Harry reluctantly climbed into the driver's seat, and by positioning myself on the bench behind a squirming Geoff we were able to keep Bambi on the straight and narrow. Luckily the road was a good one and Harry soon got the hang of our singular vehicle, though he rarely ventured above forty on the well-surfaced but rather sinuous road through a landscape that had been nothing to write home about since leaving the Burgos hills behind.

Even the approach to Cuenca was rather flat and dull, and when we passed some warehouses and entered the modern-looking town I wondered if it hadn't been a mistake to skirt much of the green part of the map. I voiced this concern when Harry had managed to find a parking space in the lower part of the town.

"Nope, the route's been just fine. We've seen plenty of mountain roads so far and I swear I can smell the sea air from here," Harry said.

"We're still at least a hundred miles from the coast."

"And I'm in no hurry to get there, not till this dratted itch goes away. I think it must be something I've eaten," said Geoff, bits of his nose now as white as snow.

"It must be psychological then," said Harry, still sniffing the air. "But I do know that I'm starving."

It being almost three o'clock, we had to find somewhere quick, so we walked into the nearest bar and ordered the daily menu, soon receiving a slap-up meal for ten euros.

"We'll have to visit the old part of town," Geoff said over coffee. "I believe those hanging houses are quite spectacular."

"Yes, we'll do that and ask where the nearest campsite is," I said.

Harry slowly raised his hand. "I have a suggestion to make."

"Go on."

"I say we stay in a little hotel tonight, just for a change."

Geoff gasped, presumably at the audacity of his suggestion.

"There's no law that says we can't sleep in a decent bed for once, and the abominable itching man here'll be tossing and turning all night because of his sunburn, so I reckon it's a good plan."

"I don't mind," I said.

"It's an allergy," said Geoff.

"Let's put what we need in your rucksack," Harry said to me, so we did, and half an hour later the two of us unpacked in our double room while Geoff took a shower in his en suite single. The hotel, or rather 'hostal', was cheap, cheerful and on the edge of the old town, so as I lay down for a much needed siesta I felt glad that Harry had asserted his right to a night within four proper walls.

8

"They're just big balconies," said Harry the next morning as we stood viewing the famous hanging houses from the Parador – a really posh hotel – on the other side of the river.

"But they hang out a long way," Geoff asserted.

"Yes, the balconies do, but balconies do that everywhere. That's why they're called balconies. The *houses*, on the other hand, are firmly plonked on top of the rock," said Harry, before stirring his expensive coffee. "I mean, the second or third-to-last flat you had in Kendal had a balcony, but I didn't see any tourists standing outside gawping up at it."

"I'm just gawping at the view in general," I said, pointing out the imposing cliffs upon which the old town was perched, plus the vertiginous iron bridge across the gorge that we had just traversed.

"Yes, it's pretty awesome, if you ignore the balconies," said Harry, who was in a fine mood after a light dinner, not much wine, and an excellent night's sleep. His snoring had woken me just the once, and it was only Geoff who hadn't benefitted from his night in a decent bed, judging by his sleepy red and white face and crabby humour.

"Oh, give it a rest, fatso," he snapped.

"I might be fat, but at least I've still got my skin to hold it in," he laughed.

"Now now, boys, let's not be falling out. I'm sure you'll sleep better tonight, Geoff, as I think the worst of it is over."

"Yes, my legs are going brown now, like I said they would."

"You'll be starting afresh on your nose tan, I'm afraid," said Harry.

"Facial skin regenerates really quickly," I said. "Are we staying at the hotel again tonight?"

"Yes," said Harry.

"No," said Geoff.

"So I have the deciding vote. I'm willing to listen to your arguments for and against, of course, but we saw the old town last night and we've checked out the gorge, so unless you want to while away the day in the abstract art museum in the hanging houses, I reckon we should head off southwards."

"I've no real interest in abstract art, and those balconies will just make me crack up laughing, so I guess I don't mind if we push off," said Harry.

"Great. Let's check out before twelve and hit the road."

The main road south from Cuenca was as well-surfaced and quiet as I'd come to expect by then, but the terrain soon flattened out and though the scenery was quite pleasant, I did feel that we'd copped out a bit by bypassing the hills to the north. After another *menu del día* lunch at a roadside restaurant near Motilla del Palancar, I pressed on – as no-one else volunteered to drive – and I soon realised that we were well and truly on the Spanish *meseta*, or plateau, where fields of vines and cereals stretched away as far as the eye could see.

"This is a bit dull," said Geoff on waking from a fitful nap.

"Yes, it is, though it's quite impressive in a way. The nearest big green patch on the map is over towards Valencia, so I think we'll turn east when we can and head towards somewhere where there might be a campsite."

"Right you are," he said, before his head lolled once more.

Harry appeared to be napping too, on the right-hand bench, so I took all the curves to the right with great care, as the ones to the left merely pinned him to the wall, and after two hours of tranquil driving along good minor roads I was relieved to see hills in the distance. There were no spectacular peaks, but they looked green enough and I was confident we'd find a campsite somewhere within that rolling terrain. The cultivated land soon petered out and we entered sparse and scrubby pine forests where I noticed that the soil had a reddish hue which I suspected was less fertile, thus the lack of clearances, though I did see some ploughed fields and a few planted with cereals here and there, but no vines, which made a change after the millions – perhaps literally – that I'd driven past. After a few twists and turns that finally roused my somnolent passengers we reached the village of Cofrentes, which at first sight seemed to be a prosperous place with a castle perched atop a rocky escarpment. I'd driven about 120 miles altogether and thought I'd done well to get us through the flatlands in so short a time.

"That castle's remarkably well-preserved," said Geoff after I'd pulled over just before entering the village streets.

"Looks restored to me," said Harry, his head now between ours. "They must have plenty of money to throw about here."

"Hmm, the village looks OK and it seems to be a nice valley. We could have a beer and ask about a campsite," I said.

"What's all that smoke over there?" Geoff asked, before jumping out and walking a little way down the road. When he clasped his hands to his head we got out and joined him.

"It's a thumping great power station," said Harry, pointing to two huge chimneys. "Strange putting that in such a pretty place."

"I guess they have to put them somewhere. I'm sure the campsite won't be in view of it. Let's walk down from here."

We found a bar just down the road and ordered beers up at the counter. When Harry had nipped to the loo – we'd agreed to space out our visits from now on – Geoff asked the unhealthy looking waiter about the grey monstrosities.

"Ah, yes, our power station," he said in Spanish. "It has been very good for the village." He smiled benignly in that direction. "Before, Cofrentes was a shithole, but since 1984 there are more jobs and more money. It supplies most of the electricity for the whole Valencian Community; about five percent of Spain's energy."

Geoff quickly translated this for me.

"I think he's exaggerating, Geoff. There are only two chimneys. Never mind, ask him about a campsite."

Geoff asked and the mottled man replied.

"He says there's one in the village of Jarafuel, a few kilometres to the east."

"Out of sight of the chimneys, I hope."

Geoff asked him something else and the man's reply made his face go even redder as he suppressed a laugh.

"What?"

"It's a nuclear power station."

"Right, that explains why it's so effective. Is there a Geiger counter in the van?"

"I'll have to check. Let's not tell Harry until we've found the campsite. He's a bit squeamish about things like that. He never liked working in Morecambe because it was that much nearer to Heysham power station. He once said that he wouldn't be surprised if he woke up one morning to find that he'd grown another head."

"A disturbing thought. He here comes, so not a word."

From the campsite on the edge of the nondescript village of Jarafuel the chimneys were barely visible, but you couldn't miss the thick plumes of vapour which cut through the view of the hillside. Camping Las Jaras consisted mainly of little wooden cabins and as they only cost about fifty euros a night we decided to stay in one, just for a change. There were quite a few occupied cabins, some of which appeared to have long-term tenants, judging by the variety of personal belongings to be seen under the little porches, and though the campsite itself had many facilities, including a restaurant, shop, pool and laundry room, it all seemed a bit unkempt and there was quite a lot of dog dirt around.

"I don't think much of this," said Harry once we'd taken possession of our rather grubby shack. "I think I'll sleep in Bambi."

"Yes, it's pretty crap and the countryside's not that special. We can get some washing done though, and then shoot off tomorrow," I said, feeling that even without the proximity of the nuclear reactors it was by far the worst place we'd stayed at so far. I mean, there were hills and plenty of trees, but it somehow looked desolate and inhospitable, maybe due to the reddish earth I mentioned.

"Hmm, for countryside you can't beat Cantabria," said Geoff. "Perhaps we should have stayed there."

"What? It was your idea to traipse all the way through Spain, you great red lump," said Harry with more than a touch of ire in his voice. He's fairly tolerant most of the time, but when he takes a dislike to something he does so with a vengeance. I hoped that Geoff would omit to mention the nuclear presence, or we'd be back on the road within ten minutes, and I doubted that the rather grumpy lady who had attended us would give us a refund.

"Cantabria was a safe bet, it's true, but we can always go back there one day," I said, weighing my words carefully. "Our trip is more of an adventure and you have to admit it's gone pretty well so far. We're bound to have at least one… less wonderful night."

"Well I'm not having dinner in this dump. We'll walk into the village and get some grub there."

"I'm up for that," said Geoff, to my relief.

I felt further relief when we'd walked the few hundred yards to the village without mention being made of the distant smokestacks, even more ominous-looking in the fading light. After the grouchy campsite woman – probably the owner – it was nice to be greeted by a friendly face when we entered a neat little bar near the surprisingly pleasant main square. We ordered some tapas and a bottle of wine from the homely young lady and soon lapsed into a brooding silence. The Ayora-Cofrentes Valley had made us rather gloomy and I hoped it wasn't a result of nuclear waste seeping into the soil. As neither of my friends seemed inclined to speak, I decided to choose a topic which might lift our spirits, or at least get us talking.

"Have you had any business ideas yet, Geoff? I asked him.

"Yes, you said you had tons of ideas," said Harry. "Let's hear one."

Geoff lifted his hand to his disfigured nose, but refrained from touching it, instead scratching his head. "Well, to be honest, over the last few days I've left it to my subconscious to process possible projects."

"And has your subconscious come up with anything yet?" I asked with an encouraging smile.

"Not as such, but I'm inclined towards something outdoorsy, or I was till I came here."

"What, like a campsite or something?"

"Yes, well, the other ones we stayed at made me think about that, but where we are now has put me off again. It's amazing how places can have such different atmospheres."

"Hmm, but the cost of a campsite would be huge," I said, disinclined to pursue the subject of atmospheres. "Though I guess you could manage one."

"You'd have to get a job at one first, to learn the ropes," said Harry, seeming disposed to be helpful rather than scathing.

"Yes, I could. Maybe I should have asked in Cantabria or Quintanar."

"I think nearer the coast would be more suitable. Being bilingual would be useful there and you'd enjoy the variety of clientele," I said.

"I speak French too, and get by in German."

Harry raised his eyebrows, but a glance from me brought them down again, as it was no time for teasing Geoff about his linguistic pretensions.

"You'll have to get a job soon, so why not try to get one in Spain?" Harry said.

"Yes, you could sort one out and then nip back to wind up your affairs in Kendal," I said. Geoff's impetuosity always had to be borne in mind and I didn't fancy emptying his flat and storing his things in my garage, something that could well happen if I wasn't careful.

Geoff chewed a squid ring pensively for a while, washed it down with a gulp of red wine, smiled and banged the table.

"Uh-oh," said Harry.

"Sí?" said the waitress.

I ordered another bottle of wine.

"Harry, you no longer have any ties, do you?" Geoff asked him with that fanatical light in his eyes for the first time since frazzling his skin.

Harry seemed to grow smaller in his chair. He opened his mouth to speak, but nothing came out, after which quite a bit of wine went in.

I rubbed my wedding ring and thought fondly of my wife June, who I'd been texting every couple of days.

"Think about it, Harry. You've retired on a good pension and you'll shortly have the proceeds from half a house... a big house," Geoff enthused.

I filled Harry's glass.

"Now's the time to do the things you dreamed about when you were stuck with Debbie for all those years."

"I dreamt about living on my own, in England."

"Pah! Why wither away in that damp and dreary climate when you could blossom anew under the Spanish sun."

I couldn't imagine Harry withering away anywhere – quite the opposite, in fact, unless he got down to doing regular exercise – but it was true that he could do worse than start afresh somewhere warm. Geoff, however, was going about things in the worst possible way, so I decided to mediate.

"I see your point, Geoff, that Harry's in a good position now to settle somewhere else, if he so desires." I turned to Harry. "Before you buy some little place in Lancaster, because I doubt you'll be able to afford anywhere out of town."

He grunted, sipped, and grunted again.

"*But*, I think it's a fatal mistake for one friend to try to convince another to do something that they haven't thought out for themselves."

Now it was Geoff's turn to grunt, sip, and grunt once more, so at least they had that in common.

"Besides, this godforsaken village is no place to talk about things like that. Wait till we get down to the coast, because I'm sure that's the place for both of you... or either of you."

"I could live in the same *place* as Geoff, but not under the same roof."

"The feeling is mutual, I assure you," said Geoff a bit haughtily.

"You must both think for yourselves and weigh up your options. Soon we'll reach the marvellous Mediterranean and a new, blue light will be cast upon things; unless you want to stay here another night, that is."

"Near a nuclear power station? No thanks," said that idiot Geoff.

"Near a *what*?"

It had taken a lot of rational argument and two large glasses of brandy to convince Harry not to jump into Bambi and flee into the night, but we'd managed to get him back to our shack, relegating Geoff to Bambi as Harry insisted on having at least a couple of layers of wood between him and the radioactive air. By nine o'clock the next morning we were well past the town of Ayora, at the end of the valley, before he deemed it safe to stop for breakfast.

"I need the toilet. There was no way I was sitting down on a bog seat back there," he said when we alighted at a roadside bar on the outskirts of Almansa.

After orange juice, toast, croissants and coffee, I opened the relevant map and handed it over to them.

"We're not far from the coast now, but you two decide how you want us to get there," I said, as my last choice of destination had not been a success.

"Straight down the motorway to Alicante, then up to Benidorm," said Harry.

"No *way* am I going to Benidorm," said Geoff as if he meant it.

"Would Bambi be all right on the motorway?" I asked. "She slows to forty on the uphills."

"Is she even *allowed* on the motorway?" asked Harry.

"She's allowed, but I have an alternative proposal," said Geoff, before suggesting that we take the main road south to Yecla and then head east into the Alicante mountains. "There are lots of roads marked with green so it must be picturesque. I reckon we should wild camp for at least one night, and I think that's the place to do it."

"I'm up for it," I said. I vaguely remembered the view inland from Javea and thought it a promising sierra, tantalisingly close to the coast.

"We'll have to buy bread, milk, wine and stuff," said Harry, which I took to be an affirmative.

"Shall we take a look at the castle here?" I asked.

"Nah, it's another of those refurbished ones," said Harry.

"You didn't want to look at the one at Ayora because you said it was too dilapidated," I protested.

"And too near to those infernal chimneys. I guess I'm just not a castle person."

"And I'm no longer a driving person." I dropped the keys onto the table. "It's my turn to be co-pilot, up front."

Geoff snatched up the keys and after refuelling drove us south to Yecla. Without entering the sprawling town we headed due east to Villena, where we popped into a supermarket, and it wasn't until we passed the village of Bañeres that the scenery began to improve, as it had been pretty dry and uninspiring until then. Geoff was making a beeline for the Alicante mountains and when we hurtled past the striking village of Bocairente I protested that we weren't exactly meandering along, taking in the sights.

"I like to meander quickly. We turn right soon onto a road that'll take us to a place called Muro de Alcoy. It's after there that the green roads begin."

A glance at the map told me that he'd memorised it well and I made the mistake of mentioning this.

"My memory's practically photographic."

"That's unfortunate, considering some of the birds you've shagged over the years," said Harry from the back.

"Beauty is sometimes in the eye of the beholder, Harry. Besides, now that you're a free man again, we'll see what kind of birds *you* pull. My aesthetic demands might have fallen ever so slightly over the years, but I'll be interested to see who you manage to grasp in those spade-like hands of yours."

"I'm not looking. Women are a strange breed and I've no intention of letting any of them get their claws into me... and my pensions."

"Never say never, Harry," I said.

"Oh, I don't, but you'll not catch me sniffing about after everything with tits like this aging lothario. I'll keep my eyes open, but nothing more than that."

"Then you'll remain alone, old man. Men always have to make the first move. It's the law of nature. Women indicate their availability and we make our choice," Geoff said as he drove past another pretty village.

I thought about Marta back in Cantabria and how Geoff had been sure that she'd had the hots for him, but that she'd actually preferred my company, in a platonic way, of course.

"Maybe when we get down to the coast and start seeing more people you'll be able to give Harry a few lessons in the art of lovemaking," I said.

"Ugh!" said Harry.

"Or rather the art of... wooing, yes, that's the word I was looking for."

"I don't mind showing him the ropes," said Geoff with a shrug. "But I doubt he'll be a willing apprentice."

"Too right I won't." He prodded his stomach. "It's time for lunch."

"We'll reach Muro at two o'clock, as scheduled."

It felt warmer when we got out of the van and as the sun was burning down I declared that I might change into shorts.

"Not before lunch, please, Jeremy. The locals will take us for tourists if you do that," said Geoff.

"What the hell do you think they'll take us for in this van and with your nose? Besides, we look English," said Harry.

"I practically passed for a local back in Jaén…" Geoff began, but Harry was already following an olfactory lead towards a busy bar a little way down the street.

Muro de Alcoy is a small town wedged between modest mountain ranges and though architecturally no different from other towns we had passed through – four or five storey blocks of flats and a few older buildings – it felt different, as if the sea, now only twenty miles away as the crow flies, was making its presence felt.

"Can you smell the sea now, Harry?" I asked when I'd caught him up.

He sniffed. "Nope, just food, but it *feels* like the sea's close."

"That's what I thought."

Geoff tapped me on the shoulder, looking excited. "We're a bit early. That shop just there's still open. It must be fate. I'll meet you in the bar," he said, before loping off in the other direction.

"That was a bit enigmatic," I said.

"Just bloody nuts," said Harry.

The waiter had just got round to taking our order when Geoff appeared with a guitar under his arm. He placed it carefully on the spare chair and made his choice from the daily menu.

"When you walked in I thought you'd grown, but I now see that it's the guitar that's a bit small," I said.

"It's a three-quarter size."

"I didn't see a music shop," said Harry.

"No, it was in the window of a stationer's. It's for youngsters really, but I thought it'd be just the thing to help us while away the evenings." He leant over to strum the nylon strings, immediately making us the centre of attention, as all our fellow customers, mostly working men, turned round to look.

"Careful, they might get the crazy idea that we're tourists," said Harry.

"You could go from table to table serenading them. They might give you something," I said.

"Like a smack on the nose, though it wouldn't make it look any worse."

We both knew that Geoff purportedly played the guitar – like the eleven-string one I mentioned earlier – but we'd never been privileged to hear him perform. As he ate his lamb stew with his spoon, he kept pawing his new instrument with his left hand, but I sincerely hoped he wouldn't begin to strum chords over coffee.

"Shall I pop it into Bambi?" I offered. "It looks a bit daft there."

"No, I'm just working out a tune in my head. I haven't played for a long time, but I'm sure I'll remember a few songs."

"Play one here and I'll bash it over your head," said Harry with a chicken bone between his teeth, making him look like a baddie from a spaghetti western, as he'd already caught the sun, as had I, though we'd both applied cream assiduously.

"What sort of things can you play?" I asked.

"Well, I dabbled in flamenco back in Jaén, but mostly old folk songs and stuff. I'll play something tonight, seeing as we're wild camping. Hopefully we'll be able to have a campfire to sit round."

"I'm not sure that'd be wise, Geoff. They have enough forest fires as it is."

"This… er, wild camping business," Harry mumbled, still munching an artichoke. "Is it strictly necessary? I'm sure there'll be campsites where we're heading."

"Oh, where's your spirit of adventure?" said Geoff.

"I haven't got one. Besides, it'll probably mean us all sleeping in Bambi, and you *know* how I snore, especially after wine, which I plan to drink a lot of."

"Let's just see how things pan out, shall we?" I said, in my habitual role of go-between. "We'll head up into those nice hills and see what we find."

Harry pointed at the guitar. "I really wish he hadn't bought that. I've a gut feeling that nothing good will come of it."

How wrong Harry was, you will see in a few days' time.

9

As Harry insisted on sitting up front for the last leg, I opened the map in the back and tried to guess which route Geoff had stored in his photographic memory. When he turned off the road towards Planes and headed south along a minor road, I pinpointed the two possible mountain passes he could take, before using my phone to take a quick look at the campsites in the area. As I said earlier, the internet was supposed to be out of bounds, but I saw no harm in checking what was available as, like Harry, I wasn't overkeen on the idea of wild camping if we didn't really have to. I imagined Bambi parked in a dusty layby and us crouching behind almonds trees to relieve ourselves, before wiping our bottoms on stones and burying our waste. Being used to my creature comforts, this didn't appeal to me.

On google maps I saw several campsites near to the coast, but one place still in the hills caught my eye and sounded like a nice compromise.

"Geoff, I think I've found the ideal spot for our wild adventure. We ought to head towards a place called Castell de Castells."

"That's the plan. The other road goes past Guadalest, and if I'm not mistaken it's a prettified village where the Benidorm hordes go on day trips to buy souvenirs and generally lower the tone of the place."

"Right, good, because near Castell de Castells there's a place called El Castellet, which is a… natural space where you're allowed to camp," I said as I perused the website.

"And how, prey, do you know that?" he asked accusingly.

"Oh, I stumbled across it on my phone. I was just texting June and…"

"Ha, so much for our anti-internet policy!"

"There's nowt wrong with that if it saves us from sleeping by the side of the road like bloody gypsies," said Harry, whose years on the force had made him no more PC than when he'd started out.

"We'll check it out," said Geoff, which pleased me as the narrow road had just become so picturesque that I didn't want to spend the next half hour trying to convince him of my choice. Having been climbing steadily – at about 20mph – for a while, it was after passing the village of Cuatretondeta that the road began to zigzag with a vengeance as it made its way past increasingly neglected fields of olive and almond trees. It began to feel really wild and isolated up there and trundling through the pretty village of Facheca only broke the spell for an instant, before the road widened slightly and began to descend into the next valley. I imagine that before the advent of tourism the score or so hamlets and villages in the sierra had been quite poor and isolated, but its proximity to the coast had brought in a new source of revenue, judging by the occasional flashy car that passed by and the signs for restaurants and rural lodgings.

The descent through pine trees to Castell de Castells was very sinuous indeed, but Geoff coaxed Bambi around each bend with great suavity, thanks to which my lunch was still where I'd stowed it when the village finally came into view. Parts of the valley were a bit drier and scrubbier than I'd expected, probably due to previous forest fires, but I still found that remote place perched part-way up the hillside charming. I suppose it wasn't a patch on Cantabria really – but then it rained a lot less – so I guess it's horses for courses and there was just something about it that really appealed to me, whereas Cantabria had merely reminded me of home.

"Why don't you come and live here?" I asked the boys up front. "I'd definitely come and visit you here."

"What makes you say that?" Geoff asked. "We haven't even seen what it's like yet."

"I don't know really. I just like the look of it. Let's stop for a beer before we find the camping place."

Geoff parked near the Hotel Rural Serrella, a large green building which looked purpose-built, and we walked up the pleasingly unbeautified street in search of a humble bar in which to quaff an ale with the locals, but after wandering around for a bit we'd only spotted two posh-looking restaurants, so Geoff asked an old man who was perusing a fine array of flowerpots if there weren't a cosy little bar where we could quench our thirst. For the sake of clarity and brevity I'll reproduce the dialogue between them as Geoff reported it to us afterwards, so please allow for his embellishments, though they did natter on for quite a while.

"A bar here?" said the dark, rather wizened oldie. "There is, but it is closed today. There used to be several, but now there are only the two restaurants and the hotel, all run for foreigners."

"Only for foreigners?"

"Oh, one can enter, if one chooses, but I don't. When one takes a wine one wishes to talk loudly and spit on the floor." He spat on the pavement. "But that is not possible in those elegant places."

"How awful. Tell me, señor, how has this fine village changed during your time here?"

"During my eighty-four years – *eighty*-four, eh – it has changed beyond recognition. Bah, before it was a place of families and of work. When I was born there were over a thousand people here – in my father's time even more than that – but now there are just five hundred souls, if you count the foreigners."

"What did everyone do, when you were young?"

"Do? What were we to do? Work the land, of course. Our almonds, olives and carob beans were the finest in the sierra and most men had a plot of land, so we had plenty to eat."

Noticing his soiled nails, Geoff asked him if he still had a piece of land.

"But of course. What is a man without land? And I work it, every day, including Sundays, at *eighty*-four, eh," he said in his gravelly voice, completing each phrase in an accusatory tone, though he appeared happy to have an audience, as he looked at each of us in turn when making an especially forceful point. "But I will be the last, as my two sons have no interest in it." He shook his head and his partially toothed mouth snapped shut in a peevish grimace.

"What do they do?"

"Do? What are they to do? They work in the city, wear suits and get fat. My eldest son is as tall as the big one." He pointed at Harry. "As tall and... one day he will be as big."

Given that the man was about five feet five and can't have weighed more than nine stone, this generational change – much in evidence all over Spain – can only be down to an improved diet, or at least an abundance of food, which made me wonder if they really had eaten so well back in the old days.

"Will either of your sons wish to keep the land?"

"Keep the land? For what? Pah, they will sell it to the foreigners, of course, who will build a big house and one of those swimming pools. Pisc*i*na," he repeated, before another jet of saliva hit the ground. (I can vouch for this, if nothing else, as I followed its trajectory.)

"Do you dislike foreigners, señor?"

"Dislike foreigners? Why would I dislike them? There are foreigners in every country in the world, and good luck to them. They come here and spend money, which is good, but…"

"But?"

"Bah, but I don't like them coming to live here. The houses are now expensive because of them, so even more people leave for the city or the coast."

"So is there nowhere here where a man can get a glass of beer?" Geoff asked, seeing an uncomprehending Harry begin to shuffle impatiently.

"There is a shop, thank God, opposite the foreigners' restaurant."

"Which one?"

"Hierbas or something." He cleared his throat but refrained from spitting this time.

"Is it owned by foreigners?"

"One of them is foreign. French or English or something. Two men, running a restaurant, eh?" He shook his head. "A man cooking, it isn't normal."

"No?"

"Not here. I must go, back to my land," he said, but remained gazing at the flowerpots after we'd taken our leave and walked away.

Geoff told us what he'd said as we made our way to the shop. "So, do you still like the place, Jeremy?"

"Yes, but not as much. The man was right, perhaps; that we should come to visit, but not to live."

"I wonder if there's a copper here. It'd be a nice little spot to work in," said Harry.

"I doubt it. They'll be based in a town somewhere, I expect," said Geoff. "You could come here and be a volunteer cop, walking the beat and keeping the peace between the locals and the interlopers."

Harry appeared to appraise the narrow street. "Hmm, I wouldn't come to a place this small. Let's get some beers, then go and find this camping paradise of Jeremy's."

After buying three litre bottles of cold beer, we made our way back down to Bambi, passing two bars on the way, both of them open and patronised by local men, though I spotted a couple of foreigners too.

"What was that old booby on about?" Harry asked. "We could've drunk our beer here."

"Don't call him that," Geoff snapped. "He was an old-school, salt of the earth guy, like some of my more mature pals back in Jaén."

"He's got a bloody selective memory."

"I think he was just trying to make a point," I said. "Come on, let's leave this hybrid place behind and head for the sierra.

The *Espacio Natural El Castellet* lies less than a mile to the south of the village and is well signposted. As Bambi laboured up the steep concrete track the woods thickened and when we arrived the piney odour and the rustling breeze were most refreshing, as it had been quite hot in the village. El Castellet is basically a large picnic area with stone tables, benches and barbecues, sinks to wash up in, and, most marvellous of all, a toilet block which was open, clean, and had paper dispensers, some with paper. There were great views of the surrounding hills and I immediately wished to convince the others to stay for at least two nights. This was what it was all about, after all; being at one with nature, not having to pay, and having a loo to sit on. Apart from us there was just one carload of people – foreigners, of course – and on Bambi shuddering to a halt they soon made off. The sight of Harry wielding two large bottles of beer might also have influenced their decision, or maybe they were leaving anyway.

"Ah, all to ourselves," I said as I weighed up the lay of the land. "Let's park over there where it's dead flat and well-shaded."

"Where am I supposed to pitch my tent?" Harry asked, scraping the sole of his trainer on the rough earth.

"Just over there, out of snoring range, if you can get the pegs in," said Geoff. "You've got an airbed, remember."

"True. I'll try a peg."

He tried banging one in and it bent.

"Gently," I said, before taking the mallet and tapping another softly until it bent. "Hmm, you might be sleeping in the van with us."

"Let me try," said Geoff, before bending a third aluminium peg. Still crouched, he looked keenly at the ground. "There's no wind to speak of, so you could just use stones. You know, wrap the guy ropes round them."

"He doesn't snore so badly," I said.

"Yes, he does. I'll find some stones."

While Geoff scratted around on an olive grove just below the perimeter of the site, Harry and I assembled the tent without much difficultly, due to his previous masterclass, courtesy of the kids. While I clipped in the inner tent, Harry pumped up the air mattress, before sliding it inside.

"There, your weight should keep the tent down," I said, though Geoff still proceeded to tie up some of his stones and tense the guy ropes, most ineffectually, in my humble, unvoiced opinion.

Harry's annex complete, he grabbed three glasses and opened a beer while I fetched the camp chairs and little table. I thought we had everything we needed until dinner time, but I was mistaken.

"Oh, don't start with that now," Harry lamented when Geoff brought out his new guitar, nursing it like a Stradivarius.

"I must get my eye in before it goes dark. I'll just run through the chords in a jiffy and then put it away for now."

Over the years Geoff had mentioned his virtuosity in a vague sort of way several times, so I fully expected to see his fingers running up and down the fretboard at an increasingly rapid rate. Instead of this, however, he laboriously placed each digit on a string up near the end of the instrument, before bringing his right hand down with a flourish.

"What the f*ck was that supposed to be?" Harry wailed, raising his hands to his ears.

"A G chord."

"Jesus, if that's a G, I'm a Chinaman," he said, shaking his head.

"Is it tuned?" I asked.

"Ah, that must be it. I'll tune it in a jiffy."

Either Geoff's jiffies are considerably longer than most people's, or he hadn't tuned a guitar for a very long time, if ever, but after a lengthy spell of trial and error his G chord began to sound vaguely musical.

"Now for a C," he said, before the hand came down again.

June plays the piano and I know more or less what a C is supposed to sound like, and that wasn't it.

"Gawd," said Harry, before refilling his glass and stomping off to a distant picnic table.

After half an hour of patient, unperturbed and distinctly ham-fisted finger placements, Geoff had mastered, or remastered, the chords of G, C, E, D and A, or so he said. Between the E and the D Harry had returned to grab another bottle from the fridge, before topping up my glass – Geoff's was almost untouched – and slinking off back into the shadows.

"Right, let's hear one quick tune, then put it away for now. This adventure is supposed to bring us together and you've scared Harry off."

"OK, well…" he said, before running through his repertoire of chords with some difficulty, caused mainly by the need to move his fingers from one place to another within a short space of time.

"I'm a tad rusty."

"It'll come. Give us a tune."

"Hmm, I've got the music to loads of songs back home, but the only one I can think of off the top of my head is Yellow Submarine."

"Play that then. We'll both sing," I said, eager to get the guitar into Bambi and Harry back into the fold.

As he strummed we sang the first verse – the only one we knew – but it didn't sound quite right. I mentioned this.

"Hmm, I think there's a minor chord or two in there, but I can quite remember…" he muttered, before resuming his chord searching trials.

"Let's sing the chorus," I said.

He began, we sang, and it sounded OK – there are only two chords – and after six or seven renditions we were cut short by an anguished howl.

"A wolf?" said Geoff.

"A Harry. Come on, put it away for now and we'll cook up some dinner."

While we 'cooked' we finished off the beer and opened a bottle of red wine. The fresh air had sharpened our appetites to such an extent that in the end we poured the contents of a can of lamb curry, one of steak in gravy and another of beans into the largest pan and stirred it into an appetizing mess. No-one felt like cooking pasta or rice, so we ate it with yesterday's bread, in order to save today's for tomorrow, if you see what I mean.

"Delicious," said Harry as he opened another bottle of wine.

"It tastes better when you cook it yourself, doesn't it?" said Geoff.

I envisioned the 'can drawer' under the bench. "Yes, and we can have about ten more meals like this, thanks to Harry's foresight," I said, before placing the plates and forks on the ground and sliding them over to the dirty pan.

"Shall I…?" Geoff said, pointing his thumb at Bambi.

"No, for God's sake, no more music tonight," Harry pleaded.

"Let's just sip a bit more wine and chill out," I said.

We did, but about half way down the third bottle Harry allowed Geoff to bring out the guitar and we all sang Yellow Submarine – mostly the chorus – several times, gradually changing the words to the following ditty.

We all live in a little off-white van,
Little off-white van, little off-white van,
We all live in a little Bambi van,
Little Bambi van, little Bambi van…

And so on. Childish, I know, but we also began to compose a new verse, though we were too fatigued to finish it that night.

There's nothing like getting up in the middle of the countryside when the sun is just peeping over the mountainside to cure a slight hangover like the one that I'd woken up with. After quenching my thirst at one of the drinking fountains dotted about the place I surveyed our new domain for a while, before returning to base camp and unzipping Harry's tent.

"Did you sleep well?" I asked upon seeing one sleepy eye observing me from his quilted cocoon.

"Like a log. It was a bit chilly though, so I put on a few more clothes." He unzipped his bag to reveal a torso even huger than usual.

"What on earth did you put on?"

"Three t-shirts and a sweatshirt, and a towel round my legs. I don't think the bag's a very good one."

"Never mind. You know now. I'll make some coffee."

Back in Bambi Geoff was humming Yellow Submarine as he pulled on his shorts, and we were soon scoffing croissants and drinking instant coffee.

"Where's the map?" Geoff asked.

"We won't need it today. I vote we stay here for another night," I said.

Harry raised his hand and Geoff nodded.

"Let's go for a really good walk," said Harry. "I need to start my exercise regime right away."

"Right. On my phone I... stumbled across three things of interest around here. There's an old Arab fortress, some interesting rock formations – some sort of arches – and some cave paintings. The fortress and the rocks are to the south, along that track, while to see the paintings we'd have to go back through the village and take the road north for a couple of miles. Which do you prefer?"

"I saw some cave paintings in Jaén," said Geoff.

"Any good?" Harry asked.

"Very primitive. Almost childish, in fact."

"Let's see the castle and the rocks then, so we can leave Bambi here," Harry said, and we both agreed. After applying sun cream, for the sky was cloudless, I offered Geoff the tube, which he half-emptied on himself, such was his desire to avoid the dermatological problem or allergic reaction that had affected him up at the Lagunas de Neila. His nose was still rather mottled, but the rest of him had more or less recovered from his mystery ailment.

If you're ever in the area and wish to follow in our ponderous footsteps, just head south on the track from the picnic area for about a mile, where it begins to zigzag up the hillside in an amusing way, though judging by his breathing Harry didn't find it as entertaining as we did. A signpost indicated the whereabouts of 'Els Arcs', two curious arches in the rock, which I duly took pictures through with the boys standing under the larger one. Another signpost led us to the Arab fortress, right on top of the mountain, from where there are great views of the surrounding hills, a large reservoir to the south, and what can only have been Benidorm just beyond it.

"There's the Med, and we'll be there tomorrow," I said.

Geoff grimaced. "But not *there* exactly."

"No, not there."

"I don't think much of this," said Harry as he inspected the scanty remains of what must have been a formidable and eminently defendable fortress back in Moorish times.

"I prefer it when they leave them alone like this," Geoff said, loosening another stone with his foot. "I wish they'd done the same with the coast. I bet the water in that reservoir is destined to shower the repulsive bodies of our compatriots when they drag themselves out of bed after their latest moronic binge."

"I prefer to admire its lovely blue colour and not worry about where it's going," I said. "Lunch?"

After eating our butties we made our way slowly back to the van. I noticed that by no means all of the trees were pines up there, as I spotted oaks, maples and what I'm pretty sure were ash trees, so maybe the vegetation was even older than the ancient citadel overlooking it. I'd thought that the Moors had been all-powerful in the Valencia area during their centuries of residence, so it surprised me that they'd seen fit to build a fortress in such an isolated spot, but I guess they didn't always agree among themselves and maybe one prince or sultan thought it expedient to shore himself up against his rivals. I didn't use to describe things in such an informal way in my history classes, by the way, but this isn't a didactic book and I'm yet to get round to delving into the history of the Moorish conquest of Iberia, though I'm sure I will one day, perhaps when I finish this account.

When we got back there were three groups of people, all Spaniards, sitting around digesting their picnics and barbecues. Geoff went off to chat to one family for a while, but Harry and I were still wary after our grilling up in the north, so we stayed near Bambi and by the time I'd mustered up the courage to approach them, they were packing up to leave.

"Good chat?" I asked Geoff on his return.

"Yes, they're from Alcoy, a big town inland from here. He's a builder and she's a junior school teacher. I think she fancied me, so I spoke mostly to him, as he's a big guy and looked a bit jealous."

"I expect you're right," I said, though I doubted that the pretty, slender woman in her late twenties would have preferred my skinny, aging friend to her bronzed, muscular husband, but there's no accounting for tastes. "You'll soon get chance to meet some women, I'm sure, once we reach the coast."

"We've no beer and hardly any wine left," said Harry, before Geoff had chance to expand on his favourite topic.

"We could have a dry night," I said.

"I've worked up a hell of a thirst on that walk," he replied.

"There's water, water everywhere, in the fountains," Geoff said.

"And it's delicious," I added.

"Like my granddad said, water doesn't really quench your thirst. I'll nip into the village."

"Yes, another walk will burn a few more calories," said Geoff.

"In Bambi. I'll get some bread too."

We were alone again that evening, apart from the brief visit of a courting couple in a car, who soon left to find a more intimate spot. We drank beer, chatted, and as if by magic the guitar appeared. Fresh tunes failed to surface in the musical part of Geoff's brain, so we worked on our version of Yellow Submarine a little more, coming up with the following verse:

In a town, where we were born,
Lived three men, who crossed the sea,
In a little off-white van,
Christened Bambi by decree.
So we drove down into Spain,
Till we found a campsite green,
And we lived beneath the trees,
In our little Bambi van...

If nothing else, this allowed us to approach the chorus in an acceptable manner, before launching into a rousing rendition of our version of it. Geoff eventually found the A Minor chord too, which pleased him no end, so all in all it was another boozy, amusing evening, very similar to those of our compatriots down in Benidorm, no doubt, though I didn't tell Geoff that.

10

"The coast, the coast, my kingdom for the coast," Geoff intoned histrionically as he drove us through the bustling town of Callosa d'en Sarrià, almost down on the coastal plain. I'd been about to suggest driving east to Javea, which I knew was lovely, but, conscious of the fact that we were already twelve days into our adventure, I thought it better to head south, as we were still an awful long way from Gibraltar and I knew there was plenty worth seeing before we finally reached there, assuming we did, as it wasn't set in stone that we had to.

"South suits me. The sooner we leave the sight of that monstrous Sodom and Gomorrah behind, the better," said Geoff.

"Yes, let's go south and find somewhere a bit less touristy," said Harry, so I switched on my phone and began to study our options.

In order to leave his least favourite resort behind as quickly as possible, Geoff made the executive decision of taking Bambi onto the autopista, a motorway with tolls.

"Hey, we'll have to pay on here," Harry protested.

"It won't be much and it'd be slow-going on the normal road. You two sit back and enjoy the views while I get the best out of Bambi."

It took her a while to get up to her maximum speed – it always did – and when 50mph had been reached it wasn't quite fast enough, judging by the queue of lorries that formed behind us while the cars whizzed past in the other lane. It was an undulating stretch of motorway, with great views of the sea, and when we slowed to below forty on one incline, the lorries trundled past and the cars had to wait their turn, after which some of them expressed their annoyance by blasting their horns in a far from friendly way, but Harry waved at them from the passenger seat all the same, only sticking two fingers up at one especially annoyed and annoying driver.

"San Juan might not be a bad place," I said from the back, still surfing away.

"Nah, let's leave this whole overbuilt bit behind us," said Geoff. "Have a look at places south of Alicante."

I did, but as the motorway – now gratis again – headed inland towards Murcia I decided to concentrate on researching the resorts south of there. La Manga sounded a bit naff, and Águilas nothing to write home about, so I suggested Mojácar, which boasted an old village inland plus a coastal resort.

"A bit too commercial for us, I think," said Geoff.

"Have you *been* there?" Harry asked him.

"Not in person, but I know people who have. A colleague at the hotel said it was f*cking brilliant – his words, not mine – and he was a congenital idiot, so I doubt it'd suit us. What's further south?"

"There are some small places down towards Almeria. I'll have a look at them…"

I searched for Las Negras and San José and was pleased to find that they were unspoilt coastal villages in the Cabo de Gata-Nijar Natural Park.

"They sound too good to be true, but let's check them out," I said, before consulting the map. "Come off at exit 487 and head towards Las Negras."

To say that the road leading from the motorway to the coast was unpromising would be to underrate the ugliness of those first few miles. After driving through the town of Campohermoso we began to pass a series of huge, plastic greenhouses in which I assumed the few Africans I spotted nearby spent their working days. The visible land was flat and arid and I prayed that things would improve when we reached the low hills away to the east. Fortunately, before passing through a nondescript village called Fernán Pérez, the plastic ceased and after a few more miles of wilderness the sea appeared over the barren hills and the road began to descend towards the bright white village. It was like reaching an oasis after miles of virtual desert and I liked what I saw. Unspoilt it wasn't, as some of the houses were clearly quite new, but there was nothing higher than three storeys and the whiteness complemented the clear blue sea so well that the aridity didn't seem to matter anymore.

"What do you think?" I asked when Geoff had managed to park about two hundred yards from the sea.

"I think it's OK, but where have all these cars come from?"

"It's Sunday, remember. I bet most of these folk have come here for lunch and will shoot off later," I said hopefully. It was after three – we'd driven almost non-stop for over five hours – and I guessed that the car owners were eating in the restaurants which proved to be surprisingly numerous for so small a place.

"I think it's bloody brilliant," said Harry. "I never expected to see a place like this in Spain."

After we'd walked down to the beach Harry's enthusiasm reached new heights of eloquence.

"Bloody hell, it's even better down here with all these little old houses."

"*This* is nothing special," Geoff said, kicking at the large pebbles on the thin strip of beach.

"You can't have everything. If there was a proper beach it'd have become like the rest of the coast. We'll be fine on our camp chairs and the sea looks so clean," I said, loving it almost as much as Harry.

Geoff liked it too, but had to make one more critical observation before admitting it.

"Strange place to designate a natural park though, isn't it? The land's bone-dry."

"I believe it's of ecological importance, but I reckon the main motivation was to stop people building. I doubt there are many places as low-rise as this on the whole Mediterranean coast," I said, breathing in the sea air. The sun was out, as usual, but it felt fresher there than back in Castell de Castells.

"Oh, there are lovely spots on the Cádiz coast too, but we won't be going that far," said Geoff.

"Have you *been* there?" Harry asked.

"Yes, as a matter of fact I have. Carmela and I spent a wonderful week down there, quite near Cape Trafalgar. That was just before the thumbscrews began to tighten and I had to hop it."

"I'm hungry and thirsty," said Harry.

"We're a bit late for lunch, I'm afraid," I said.

"Nonsense, at the beach they're more flexible," said Geoff, before proving it by leading us to a restaurant on the southern edge of the village, right by the sea, where a sweaty, dishevelled young waiter told us they could knock up a seafood paella within half an hour.

"I hope he's not being exploited," Geoff said with a frown.

"Who cares?" said Harry, beginning to salivate, I think. "We'll give him a great tip anyway for getting us this table outside *and* in the shade."

Our beers arrived while the other diners – almost all Spaniards – were drinking coffee, and by the time our paella arrived most people had left.

"This is the life," said Harry after two beers, half a bottle of white wine, and about two kilos of rice.

"This *is* the life indeed," Geoff agreed, similarly replete.

"A nice little place, eh?" I said, ever so pleased with my fortuitous choice of destination. "Where are we going to sleep?"

"In Bambi, and my tent, near the beach," said Harry decisively.

"It's not allowed. I saw a sign," said Geoff.

"Oh, bollocks. There'll be no police here," said Harry, whose attitude to law and order had been markedly different since leaving the boat. By now we rode in the back of Bambi without a care in the world, though I had ducked a couple of times when I'd seen a cop car. As I said, with a camping chair wedged between the benches and the backs of the front seats within grasping distance it seemed fairly safe, and we never reached vertiginous speeds, though I would not of course recommend it and I dread to think what June will say when she reads this.

"No, Harry, the lane along the beach is strictly no parking. There were no cars, never mind camper vans," I said.

"Is Bambi a camper van or a motorhome?" Geoff asked with astonishing irrelevance.

"That's a matter of semantics we can discuss later, but I vote we check out the campsite. It's only a mile or so south of the village, so we can drive over there now."

"I can't move," said Harry, tapping his taut belly.

"Another coffee then. Have you put cream on your nose?" I asked Geoff, because by then the sunlight was streaming in beneath the awning.

"Oh yes, I'll soon be my old handsome self again. I hope there are some nice birds at the campsite."

"What do you have in mind?" I asked.

Oh, maybe a childless Swedish divorcee. Slim, blonde, about thirty-two or so, with plenty of money and an enquiring mind."

"Fat chance," said Harry.

"There'll be someone. I can feel it in the air. Watch and learn, old man."

"Ha."

Our meal was unexpectedly cheap considering the excellent food and prime location, and the exploited waiter seemed ever so pleased with the twenty euro tip that Harry gave him.

"Thank you, come back soon," he said.

"If you speak Spanish, we will," Geoff said in Spanish.

"Como quieras," he said – as you wish – before slipping the note into his shirt pocket and giving us a jaunty salute.

Camping La Caleta is set back from a charming caleta, or little cove, and extends up into the arid hills. There were many little bungalows, some near the beach and others on the hillside, but as the camping pitches were all shaded with awnings we booked two of those, room enough for Bambi, Harry's tent, and our table and chairs in between. The friendly young chap who attended us explained that he'd been able to give us one of the better spots as the weekend was over, but that we might have to move if we stayed for over five nights, due to previous bookings.

"Oh, I don't think so," I said. "We're travelling the length of Spain, you see."

"In that?"

"Yes, in that."

"You are brave men," he said solemnly, before explaining when the shop and restaurant were open.

When Harry had pitched his tent to his satisfaction and bent a few more pegs – though he didn't bother with the guy ropes – we strolled down to the sandy beach and up along the cliffs to the south for a while, before returning for our much needed showers, as the day before we had merely sluiced ourselves at the washing up sinks. Geoff took a dip in the oval swimming pool first, and though he was the only bather he told us that if there were any eligible women on the campsite, that would be the place to meet them.

"Tomorrow we'll see what's what," he said as we sipped a beer on the restaurant terrace near the pool, as although we'd decided to skip dinner, all that rice had made us thirsty.

"How long are we staying for?" Harry asked.

"How long do you reckon?" I said, looking from one to the other.

"That depends," Geoff said with a leer, though so far I'd seen no eligible females. The site appeared to be about half full, mostly of families and couples who seemed pretty self-sufficient, as there were few people in the restaurant.

"I vote for at least three nights, regardless of Geoff's sexual fantasies," Harry said to me. "We've been together for a long time and I'd like to do my own thing for a bit."

"Like what?" Geoff asked.

"You know, just potter round on my own. Walk, swim, have a beer, not see you for a few hours."

"That suits me," I said, as a similar idea had crossed my mind and I was glad that Harry had said it first. "After breakfast tomorrow we'll split up and meet again at dinner time. It'll do us good to have a break from each other, as we've still a long way to go."

"OK, but when you get back just check that I'm not in Bambi with a new lady friend," said Geoff.

"We'd see her bouncing up and down, wouldn't we?" said Harry.

"We might be having a short rest."

"Er, don't be too indiscriminate, Geoff," I said, as I feared that left to his own devices he would comb the village in search of anything in a skirt or shorts.

"Course not. I'm not desperate. I thought Harry might want a masterclass, but if he prefers mooching about on his own, that's fine."

The trouble with Geoff, though he's a great bloke and a loyal friend, is that he's not fond of spending time on his own. Being an extrovert he always seeks the company of others, which explains his almost unbroken series of relationships with women over the years, most of them doomed to failure from the start, due to a lack of common ground and shared interests. Had we been in a large resort I'm sure he'd have formed some sort of liaison if left alone for long enough, and though that would be fine had we been staying at a hotel – in separate rooms – I didn't want him to shatter our tenuous harmony by bringing some weird woman into our midst. Still, I was pretty confident that in such a small and family-oriented place even he wouldn't be able to score, though it wouldn't be for want of trying.

Back at the van Geoff strummed the guitar quietly, but we felt too tired to sing Yellow Submarine again, besides not wishing to make a nuisance of ourselves. He soon lay down the guitar and we sat in silence for a while, before Harry began to hum the tune to Wandering Star. He has a deep, pleasant voice and in the evening calm I found it quite soothing.

"Do you know the words to that?" I asked.

"Hmm, I think so, yes. I used to sing it to Debbie, when we still enjoyed each other's company."

"A long time ago?"

"Oh, before our lad was born."

"How old's Paul now?"

"Twenty-nine next month. Let's see…

I was born under a wandrin' star,

I was born under a wandrin' star.

Wheels are made for rolling,

mules are made to pack…" and he went on with the song, very quietly, until both Geoff and I were mesmerised.

"I wonder what the chords are," Geoff whispered, reaching for the guitar.

"Oh, I don't think we need–" I began, but to no avail.

Fortunately Geoff strummed even more quietly than Harry sang, leaning over the strings and nodding when he got a chord right. I mention this because I think that if Geoff hadn't insisted on Harry singing the song twice more in order to try – and fail – to work out the chords, his initial rendition would have been the only one. The importance of this rather pedantic account will soon become apparent.

The next morning, after a healthy breakfast in the restaurant – bacon, eggs and chips – Geoff was the first to head off into the great unknown, followed closely by Harry. Left alone for the first time in almost a fortnight, I just sat there beside Bambi for a while, enjoying my liberty, before I headed off through the village and up the coastal path for a good, brisk walk. After about an hour I reached the Cala San Pedro, a sandy cove where I saw some hippy-like people knocking about and also a few nudists, who might have been hippies too, but it was hard to tell. Being a bit of a prude, the nudists put me off bathing, so I walked up to look at the crumbling remains of a castle and saw that a few people were camping nearby and had been for a while. Though it was fairly quiet during my brief visit, I believe that the cove gets packed with bohemian types in summer, which the authorities must tolerate, despite the 'no camping' and 'no fires' signs. You can get there by boat from Las Negras, by the way, but I walked back along the same path and took some photos of the curious fan palms and snapdragons. I believe it's a haven of birdlife, but my untrained eye saw only gulls, larks and a single eagle, though flamingos and other waders are said to abound in the area too.

As the weekenders had gone from the village, I noticed that it too had a slightly bohemian feel and a few of the buildings certainly had a seventies look about them. I ate a simple meal in one of the cheaper restaurants, but the truth is that the other members of my party were having a more interesting time, as I was to discover later, after I'd swum in the sea, sunbathed on the beach, had a dip in the pool, and finally returned to camp, fatigued but content after my healthy, solitary day.

An hour later, at about half past eight, Geoff appeared, looking a little the worse for wear.

"Good day?" I asked.

"Fair to middling," he mumbled, having clearing imbibed a little more than was good for him, though the booze had made him far from euphoric.

I told him what I'd done and waited for him to explain the reasoning behind his daytime session, for I was sure he'd come up with a good excuse for it. He just sat there for a while, looking at the ground with pursed lips, until I began to rise from my chair.

"A merry dance," he finally muttered, so I lowered myself back into listening position.

"What was?"

"What the silly little cow led me on… a merry dance." He shook his head and looked at me. "Rather not talk about it."

"It's better to tell me than wait for Harry to come back, as he's sure to take the piss out of you if you've done anything daft."

"True. You're a good friend, Jeremy. You know that, don't you?" He reached over to pat my leg, but just scraped my knee.

"Yes, tell me what happened."

"Oh, the age-old story... met a feisty young piece this morning, wined her and lunched her... then more drinks... not my type really, bit of a hippy... but she was coming on strong and said we'd be going back to hers later, later, later..." His voice tailed off and his head began to drop. "*But*," he cried, making me jump. "Later never came. Who did come was her damned long-haired bloke."

"And he whisked her off?"

"Hmm, but not before he'd drunk my health, at my expense... didn't know he was her bloke... few more drinks... then he jumped up, patted my *head*, and they walked off, arms round each other, laughing... never been so humiliated... better not tell Harry, eh?" he concluded with an imploring look.

"No, we'd better not," I said, realising that he really did feel demeaned by the experience. "Why don't you turn in now and sleep it off? I'll tell him you've walked for miles and were exhausted."

"You're a good friend, Jeremy. You know that, don't you?"

"Yes, now nip to the loo and then get yourself to bed. Don't worry, Harry won't know a thing."

"Good man." He pushed himself up.

"And try to walk straight. It's a family site."

He managed to get there and back without weaving too much and closed Bambi's rear door behind him in the nick of time, as a minute later Harry came striding towards me. Unlike Geoff or myself, he still had a spring in his step, so I assumed he hadn't spent the day drinking or hiking.

"What did you get up to?" he asked me before sitting down.

I gave him a brief account of my day, but he seemed inordinately interested in my activities, as no sooner had I answered one question than he made another enquiry about my fascinating outing. After a while I began to suspect that he didn't wish to discuss his own doings.

"How about you, Harry?" I finally asked.

"No sign of Geoff yet?"

"Yes, he's just gone to bed. He said he'd walked for miles and was done in. So, what…"

"That's not like him. I thought he was unfatig… undefat…"

"Indefatigable? Yes, but not today. Are you going to tell me what you've been up to, or what?" I looked at him sternly and he turned to examine Bambi's wing mirror.

"Do you fancy a beer and a bit of dinner?"

"Yes."

"I'll just get changed and we'll go to the restaurant," he said, before climbing into the van.

I was pretty perplexed by this time and wondered what on earth he'd been doing. As he couldn't have walked far or drunk much, and as the village is tiny, I conjectured that he might have taken a boat trip or even been snorkelling or something, though his tightly rolled towel had still looked dry. Was it possible that he'd returned to the van during the day and just lazed around? That would explain why he had no news, but surely he would have just said so. When he emerged a while later dressed in his clean jeans and a peach-coloured short-sleeved shirt I was more baffled than ever, as of the three of us Harry is the least inclined to fasten more buttons than are strictly necessary.

"Bloody hell, I don't know how far Geoff walked, but he must have stopped at every bar on the way. It *stinks* of booze in there."

"Yes, I think he had a couple on the way back. Come on, it's our turn now."

Not until the frosted tankards of beer were before us did Harry begin to unburden himself of his surprising news. It transpired that after walking the kilometre or so to the village he'd stopped off at a café terrace to rest his legs and hydrate himself for the longer walk he planned to take. A short time later a lady whose face, he said, rang a bell sat down at an adjacent table and wished him good morning in slightly accented English. He'd returned the greeting and soon found himself chatting to the pleasant woman, who then revealed that she was staying at the same campsite, a few pitches away, with some friends. She told him that she'd heard him singing Wandering Star and had popped out of her tent to see who was crooning in such a deep and lovely voice. She then confessed that on seeing him leave the campsite she'd followed him to the village in the hope of bumping into him.

"She isn't some weird stalker, is she?"

"Not at all. She's a lady called Laura from Belgium. She's come to see some friends from home who're on holiday here, but she's been living in a village near Malaga for about four years. She's a widow, with three grown up kids," Harry said, holding my increasingly enthralled gaze.

"Am I to assume that you've taken a liking to this Belgian lady?"

"Well, yes, I suppose I have. We really hit it off, you see. We ended up having lunch together before she met up with her friends, a nice couple."

"What's she like? How old is she?"

He looked at his watch. "You'll see in about an hour. I'm sort of glad that Geoff's out of action, as it's your opinion I'm interested in really."

"Right, well I'll wait with bated breath."

"Let's get some grub. She's eating with her pals."

An hour later, after a light dinner washed down by an unusually small amount of beer, a plump lady of average height approached our table. She looked about fifty and though not exactly pretty she had a pleasant, rosy face and a charming smile. Her short, dark hair suited her, as did her casual but stylish attire of loose-fitting beige slacks and a white blouse. We stood up and she gave Harry two unhurried kisses while lightly grasping his arm. I held out my hand, which she ignored as she planted two briefer kisses on my cheeks.

"Ha, when in Spain," she said with a laugh. "You must be Jeremy."

"Yes, pleased to meet you, Laura," I replied, charmed by her open face and resonant voice. I'd noticed that she made sure that Harry could see her mouth when she was speaking, so she was already aware of his slight deafness. Her English was almost perfect and I guessed she would speak Spanish just as well, which proved to be the case, as well as French, Flemish, German and Italian. Laura had worked in the Belgian diplomatic service, as had her defunct spouse, and culturally she was certainly a cut above my down-to-earth friend, but I won't get ahead of myself.

As she ordered a gin and tonic, Harry and I plumped for whisky rather than more beer, and we were soon chatting away like… not exactly old friends, but with a certain fluidity that came fairly easily to me and to which Laura was more than accustomed, given her professional background. Harry, on the other hand, might well have clamped up a bit under normal circumstances, as his tongue isn't especially silvery, but with Laura he was more relaxed and eloquent than I'd ever seen him in the presence of a woman, including his ex-wife. The few hours they'd spent together had clearly been enough to cement their friendship and I had a feeling even then that they'd end up being much more than pen pals.

Call it love at first sight or what you will, but one cannot deny that fate had played a part too, in the form of his repeated renditions of Wandering Star, as it later emerged that only a short time after she'd begun to eavesdrop from her tent, he sang the chorus for the last time. That was down to Geoff and his guitar, of course, but I was still glad he was snoozing away during our first meeting, as any unfortunate comments that he might well have made would not have gone down at all well with the love-struck giant.

Dash it all, you might now be thinking. This entertaining/stirring/foolish/plodding/boring (take your pick) tale is now going to descend into a soppy love story only half way into the trip, but never fear, because Harry's chance encounter with Laura will soon take a backseat, but not just yet. On finishing my whisky I left the lovebirds to it, and after thoroughly airing Bambi I crawled into bed beside my comatose companion, feeling well-pleased by the events of the day, apart from poor Geoff's somehow apt comeuppance, of course, though I was sure he'd bounce back within a day or two.

11

"I had a good laugh yesterday," Geoff said the following morning, looking only slightly peaky after over ten hours' sleep. "I drank a bit too much, but I had a really good day with a young couple who've been living here for a while." He avoided my goggling eyes. "What did you get up to, Harry?"

"I met a nice lady called Laura. You'll meet her at some point and if you make any stupid comments you won't have to worry about your nose anymore because you won't have one," he said, his voice ominous but his face placid.

Geoff's Adam's apple moved down about an inch. "Right you are, Harry. I look forward to meeting her. What are we doing today and when are we planning to move on?"

I looked at Harry.

"I reckon we should stay for one more night. Do you fancy going kayaking? There's a place in the village that hires them out, Laura told me, and after a quick lesson you can go off wherever you like, within reason."

"Is Laura coming?" Geoff asked.

"No, I'm meeting her later for dinner."

"I like the sound of kayaking, but are you sure you don't want to stay here for longer?" I asked Harry.

"No, we'd better press on as we've more places to see."

"Right. I just thought you might want a bit more time to... you know."

"No need. Laura and me have got to know each other pretty well already. We could call in and see her when we get down Malaga way, but we don't have to. She's coming over to see me next month anyway," he said in an admirably matter-of-fact way.

"My, my, you don't hang around, do you?" said Geoff, truly impressed.

Harry shrugged. "It's just the way it's worked out. So, are we all up for a bit of kayaking?"

We both agreed that it was the ideal way to spend our last full day in Las Negras, so after breakfast – just coffee for Geoff – we walked to the village and found the premises of *Buceo Las Negras*, which caters for divers, kayakers and those sedentary folk who just wish to hire a motorised dinghy, with or without skipper. A pleasant young chap called Pablo greeted us and led us down the beach to see the vessels at our disposal.

"So it's a two and a one, or a three," I said, pointing at the yellow triple kayak which I thought our best option.

"Have you kayaked before?" Pablo asked.

"A couple of times, on a lake," I said.

"Nope," said Harry.

"Yes, I've done quite a bit, so I know how to handle one of those," said Geoff, somehow managing to look pale, despite his second tan in a fortnight.

This said, Pablo handed us our lifejackets and paddles and told us we had until two o'clock – almost four hours – to paddle wherever we wished.

"Can you recommend a route?" I asked.

He examined the motley crew. "Well, don't go straight out into the sea. I think it is best that you go north. You can go as far as Cala San Pedro, I think. You will see nice cliffs and another little cove about half way there. Would you like to take snorkels?"

"No," said Harry.

"Why not?" I asked.

"I prefer not to see what's under me."

"I will get you two," said Pablo. "Oh, do you have food and water?"

"Er, no," I said.

"Well, there is at least one little bar open at Cala San Pedro, but I will get you a bottle of water," he said, before jogging up the narrow beach to his premises.

As I told Geoff that I'd been to Cala San Pedro the day before I found myself suppressing an urge to laugh.

"What?" he said.

"Oh, it's a beach where the hippies hang out, though I doubt there'll be many."

"Let's go south," he said.

"No, I want to see that ruined castle you mentioned, Jeremy," said Harry.

"Tell you what. I'll nip to the nearest bar and buy some bocadillos to take with us, then we can stop wherever we want, or eat them in the boat," I said, and headed off before Geoff could protest.

Twenty minutes later we'd taken off our trainers and pushed our kayak into the pristine water. When I say kayak I use the term loosely, as ours was a wide, open-plan type of boat that even we would find difficult to capsize.

"I'll take the back seat, so I can keep an eye on your paddling style," said Geoff, so I sat up front in order to keep us on an even keel.

"Don't go far out," were Pablo's last words after he'd seen our initial, totally uncoordinated efforts.

Beyond the tame, breaking waves, the sea was as smooth as could be, and the partially clouded sky helped to keep us cool, as did the constant spray of water that Harry managed to create.

"You're out of time, Harry," bellowed our cox-cum-captain. "Watch Jeremy's strokes and try to do the same, preferably with the paddle in the water."

We soon got the hang of it and after moderating our initial rather frantic efforts found ourselves heading slowly but surely northwards, about a hundred yards from the shore. Once we'd left the village beach behind we rounded a headland and it suddenly felt a little scary to be edging along a rocky coastline with no apparent landing places. It wasn't long before a cove came in to view, however, so I suggested heading in to take a breather.

"Suits me," said Harry.

Geoff said nothing, having remained silent since his initial spate of commands. On grounding our craft on the pebble beach, Harry and I hopped off to pull it to safety, but our task was made harder by Geoff's continued presence on the rear seat.

"Get off, you numpty," said Harry.

"Are you OK?" said I.

"Yes, sorry, just feeling a bit queasy after yesterday's excesses," said our frail skipper as he pushed himself up.

"Ha, don't tell me you're seasick already," Harry said with a chuckle.

"Of course not. I put away a lot of drink yesterday with… my friends."

"Have a bite of your sandwich. You've got nothing in your stomach," I said.

"Later," he said, before lowering himself to the ground, where he stayed while Harry and I strolled around a bit. Pablo later informed us that it was Cala Hernández where we'd broken our journey. There was nobody about that day, so it might be a good place for solitary sunbathing in midsummer, as the pebbles are sure to put many people off.

Cala San Pedro, on the other hand, which we reached less than an hour later, is far sandier and must get pretty busy in the holidays when all the gainfully employed bohemians and nudists take some time out and meet up with likeminded folk. There were no more than a score of people there when we arrived, about half of them with clothes on.

"Maybe your drinking buddies from yesterday will be here," Harry said to a still silent Geoff after he'd failed to help us ground the kayak once more.

Although I'd kept my promise and uttered not a word to Harry about Geoff's heroic failure of the previous day, I was sure he smelt a fish and had he not been besotted by Laura I'm certain he'd have probed the enfeebled philanderer until he'd got something approaching the truth out of him. Geoff just stood there forlornly, as while he certainly did not wish to bump into the wicked hippy and her opportunistic consort, nor did he feel up to suggesting a speedy turnaround, as there was no doubt by this time that he was indeed feeling seasick. Compassion is one of my greatest virtues, unless I'm feeling mischievous, but given that Harry was riding high on a wave of requited love, I took pity on my ill-used pal and suggested that he sit down to rest while I showed Harry the castle.

"Is there a way back overland," he murmured while Harry's head was obscured by his t-shirt – he was taking it off, not hiding his face from the mostly misshapen nudists.

"Yes, I walked it yesterday. It takes about an hour... and a half."

"Will you two be able to get back without me?"

"Yes, I expect we'll manage," I said, given that his paddling contribution had waned to practically zero during the course of our voyage. "Take the some water and your sandwich. You're bound to feel hungry once you start feeling less... unwell."

Harry overheard this exchange, but rather than stretching his mouth into a demonic smile, he tutted sympathetically and wished him a speedy recovery. Maybe he didn't want to risk jinxing his own good fortune by laying into the weakened warrior, or perhaps he feared that Geoff would try to get his own back by enlightening Laura regarding his shortcomings – such as his mild misanthropy, latent racism and huge appetite for beer – though I was fairly sure that even a Geoff firing on all cylinders wouldn't dare to cross him at such a decisive point in his auspicious liaison with his Belgian sweetheart.

Harry's tolerance didn't stretch to a feeling of empathy towards some of the other male patrons of the beach, however – he referred to them as good-for-nothing chimps – so after a quick look at the castle ruins he said he'd prefer to scoff his butty on the pebbly beach on the way back, so that's what we did, but not before I'd persuaded him to pull on a snorkel and take a peek at the seabed from some way off shore. There were a lot of small fish, none of which I can name, and though the water was wonderfully clear, neither of us got deep enough to observe the more minute marine life which must abound there. Proper diving would have to be undertaken to get a really close look, and as I still felt that he might appreciate more time with Laura, I suggested that we try that the following day.

"I'm not like Geoff, Jeremy," he said with a mouthful of bread and potato omelette. "If he pulled a bird he'd want to keep us hanging round till he'd had his fill, but like I said, Laura and me already know what we want, so one day more or less makes no odds."

"You didn't tell me what you'd both decided on, actually."

He freed up his mouth and swigged from the bottle of water. "Well, we're going to be together as soon as we can."

"Where?"

"Hmm, after she's seen Lancaster, and especially where I'm living now, I expect she'd prefer me to come over here."

"And would you like that?"

"Course I would. Mind you, I'd quite like us to drop in to see her on our way past Malaga, if you don't mind. She's got a house in a village in the hills with room enough for all of us. It'd be nice to stop over for a night."

"I'd be delighted, and I'm sure Geoff would too."

"I'll introduce him to her later when she picks me up. We're having dinner in the village."

"Great."

There was a certain sense of anticipation in the air that evening as the three of us sat in our camp chairs, waiting for Laura to whisk Harry off to dinner. Had he been more gregarious he might have introduced us to her friends – a couple of about her age, fifty-two, in a posh motorhome – but I for one was happy with his isolationist approach, as we might all have ended up dining together when what he really wanted was to whisper sweet nothings to his new love. Laura was camping in a modest green tent, and though I assumed she must be comfortably off, I was still surprised when she rolled up in an impeccable Mini Clubman – one of the German ones, not a real Mini.

She gave Geoff two kisses before flashing her winning smile and telling him that Harry had told her all about him.

"Ha, all good things, I hope," he said, almost totally recovered from his hangover and seasickness.

"Of course. He tells me that you're a fluent Spanish speaker and know the country well."

"Sí, claro."

"And that you lived in Jaén some years ago."

"Sí, es mi patria querida," he said, meaning 'my dear homeland'.

"I expect you know Malaga well too. Do you know a village called Canillas de Albaida, in the mountains north from Torrox?"

"Er, let me see… no, I believe I don't recall it."

"Well, that's where I live and I hope you'll come to stay with me for a couple of nights on your way to Gibraltar."

"That's very kind of you, Laura. We'd love to," I said before Geoff could express even the tiniest shadow of doubt.

"Excellent. I leave here in two days' time and will be driving straight back, so your rooms will be ready for you when you arrive."

Her use of the plural pleased me, as it would be a treat to sleep alone for once, and in a proper bed.

"We must go now. I've booked a table for half past nine. I will bring Harry back safely," she said with a giggle, before they climbed into the nifty red and black motor and rolled away.

"What do you think?" I asked Geoff.

"I prefer the Mini Paceman, personally."

"Not the car, stupid, Laura."

"Oh, yes, she seems like a pleasant old thing. Wouldn't suit me, of course, but all things considered I think Harry's done all right for himself," he said, a shrug punctuating each phrase.

"I'd say he's done damn well for himself. She's an intelligent, stylish woman, and though money's not the main thing, I've a feeling she's got plenty of it."

"A bit on the dumpy side though. I wonder if she's got any nice dau–… nieces."

"You never know. If you behave yourself, your visit to her house could open up a new circle of friends for you."

"*Bel*gian friends?" he said, wrinkling his refurbished nose.

"Yes, and Spanish too, as she's been living in the village for four years. You don't mind us going there, do you?"

"No-oh, but it's hardly in keeping with our spirit of adventure, is it?" he said, just being awkward for the sake of it, I knew.

"If you remember, part of your adventure consists of finding something to do with yourself. Laura might have some contacts that could be useful."

"I doubt it. Business is a man's world in Spain, but I'm open to suggestions. Let's go and get some dinner. I'm starving."

"We could delve into Harry's store of tins and maybe combine a couple."

"Yuck," he said, before pointing in the direction of the restaurant.

I took the Andalucia map along and over coffee we tried to decide where to go next. To follow the coast would be the logical route, but I remembered what the friendly cyclist had said on the boat about the Alpujarras. That would mean skirting Almería and following a road parallel with the coast but at least twenty miles away from it, separated by a mountain range. After the peace of Las Negras I didn't fancy moving on to a more built-up resort, and the sinuous road through curiously named villages stirred my imagination, so I resolved that Geoff would persuade me to go through the Alpujarras.

"There are plenty of places to visit on the coast on the way to Laura's," I began. "There's Almeria, which you already know, and tons of other places. What do you think?" I turned the map to face him.

"Hmm. Let me see. I know that in El Ejido they grow vegetables under miles of plastic, so that's out. Adra sounds OK and Almuñécar rings a bell, though I believe Nerja gets a few too many Brits for my liking," he said, tipping his head from side to side in a sagacious sort of way, though he knew the places as well as I did, from the map.

"Ha, that crazy cyclist on the boat said something about going through somewhere called the Alpujarras, but I don't suppose that's a good idea."

"Hmm, the Alpujarras, that is…" He waved his finger above the map.

"Along here."

"Ah, yes, of course."

"There are a lot of roads marked green on the map, so it must be pretty along there, but I guess we've dragged Bambi up enough mountain roads by now. I expect she'd prefer to cruise down the main road or the motorway."

"Hmm, Órgiva, Cádiar, Ugíjar," he said, sounding like he was masticating pebbles. "They're all familiar to me, but I can't quite place them now."

'Because you've never been there,' I thought.

"I think the coast will be easier," I said.

"Yes, easier and more predictable. I think we should give the Alpujarras a shot. We can always drive down through Berja to the coast if we don't like what we see."

"Maybe Harry will prefer the coastal route though, as it'll be quicker. He'll be dying to see Laura. I don't think they've… done anything yet, unless he's been tent creeping."

"He'll just have to wait to bed his chubby little Laura then, won't he? Are you with me on this one, Jeremy?"

"Oh, all right then."

The following morning Laura came over to see us off, and judging by the way she hugged and kissed Harry they'd already become quite intimate, though when they'd returned at just after twelve I'd heard him unzip and re-zip his tent and begin to snore soon afterwards, so he either slept alone or she's not an over-demanding lover. Harry was all for the Alpujarras, and as Geoff and the love of his life had almost been pickpocketed on their visit to Almeria twenty-odd years earlier, he had no wish to revisit the city when it came into view.

"The sneaky sod shoved his hand into Carmela's handbag, so I was forced to restrain him," he said, rubbing his knuckles on the steering wheel.

"Did you duff the bastard up?" asked Harry eagerly.

"No, a blow to the solar plexus was enough, and the rest of the gang scarpered."

"Big lads, were they?" Harry asked.

"Not especially *big*, but the one I hit was at least eighteen, I'd say."

Bearing in mind Geoff's habitual exaggeration, I guessed he'd probably cuffed an urchin and sent him packing, but the thought of him with his old flame made me turn to the upper half of the map.

"You know, Geoff, it's not a million miles to Jaén from the western end of the Alpujarras. About… eighty, in fact. We could drive up there if you like."

"No, no, it'd bring back too many memories."

"What's wrong with that?" Harry asked.

"Nothing, but it's out of our way. You'll be keen to see Laura anyway."

"A couple of days either way make no odds to me. You could look up all your old pals… and maybe even Carmela," he said with no discernible hint of mischief in his voice.

"Oh, no, I wouldn't want to do that. I mean, she must be nearly fifty now." He shook his head. "I prefer to remember her as she was then, the perfect dark-haired, brown-eyed, olive-skinned Andaluz beauty."

"You're forgetting something, Harry, and you too Geoff," I said from the back, before focussing my voice on the nape of Geoff's neck. "Remember that you did a runner to escape the bonds of matrimony. I believe they're big on honour around here, so they might still want to lynch you for leaving her."

"Did you get her up the spout?" Harry asked.

"Of course not. I mean, I was careful even then. Jeremy has a point though. I doubt they'd be so rancorous, but you never know, and I bet her brothers still pack a punch, not to mention all the shotguns they've got. No, all things considered I think it's best if we give Jaén a miss. Do we go left up ahead?"

"Yes, follow the signs to Alhama de Almeria," I said, glad to be leaving the busy main road and the sporadic horn tooting that we'd almost got used to by then.

The scenery so far had been incredibly arid and I remembered Frank the cyclist mentioning the Almeria desert. Though we didn't penetrate the driest terrain – where they filmed the Spaghetti Westerns in the sixties – we still got a taste of the alarming desertification that is making inroads into south-eastern Spain. It wasn't until we were well beyond Alhama that more trees began to appear, but the mountains up ahead looked pretty barren.

"If these are the Alpujarras I don't think much of them," said Harry, echoing my thoughts.

"It's got to get better," I said, hoping that Frank hadn't seen the place through green-tinted specs.

It did get gradually greener, but not until we reached the large village of Láujar de Andarax did the scenery begin to show any real promise. Later research told me that Láujar sits right in the middle of the Alpujarras and that the Eastern Alpujarras are trying to get in on the rural tourism act that has made the western part better known to us, due to the book *Driving Over Lemons,* a vigorous marketing campaign and, above all, the true merits of the *Western* Alpujarras, though Láujar isn't a bad little place.

We finally stopped for lunch in the small white town of Ugíjar, which sits in a wide, fertile valley. Though the Sierra Nevada can be seen to the north, it's quite a distance away and I had a feeling that any campsites would be up that way, which proved to be the case, as a helpful chap in the restaurant told us the nearest one was at Laroles, about half an hour to the north. This meant retracing the last few miles, but when the new road began to rise relentlessly into the high hills I felt a tingle of anticipation; a feeling, or tingle, which Geoff, of course, didn't admit to sharing.

"This is hard work for Bambi and hardly seems worth it. Maybe we should have gone along the coast like I said."

Though this was a barefaced lie, it was true that the gradient was tough on our trusty van and it was a relief when an overtaking lane appeared, especially for the dozen or so cars and vans that had been crawling along behind us. The village of Laroles appeared suddenly round a bend and disappeared just as quickly as we continued up the road. At first sight *Camping Alpujarra* appeared to be a dump, due mainly to the hand-painted sign on what looked like an extremely shabby reception building.

"I knew it," said Geoff.

"It'll do," said Harry.

"Let's see," I said, crossing my fingers.

Once past the now redundant building, however, it proved to be a pleasant, terraced site among the trees which offered the usual wooden cabins, plenty of camping pitches, a large pool, a gurgling hot tub, a restaurant, and even a trampoline which I urged Harry not to try out, no matter how buoyant he was feeling.

"I might have a go though," said Geoff.

"There's probably an age limit," I said.

"Or a weight limit. In that case you'll be all right," said Harry, slapping him lightly on the back.

We booked a double pitch and, like at Las Negras, used the middle bit as our social space. Conscious of the danger of becoming repetitive, and as nothing noteworthy occurred during our two-night stay at the campsite, I won't bore you with all the details of our time there, save to say that we did a lovely walk up towards the Sierra Nevada, which hardly seemed to get any nearer despite an outward leg of about two hours. We enjoyed a jacuzzi after that and I also managed a few lengths of the very chilly pool. The restaurant provided adequate meals, but its main charm was the spectacular views to be had from there, especially at sunset when the sky turned rosy over the mountains to the south and west. We had a relatively healthy time during our stay, as Harry, the main instigator of immoderate alcohol consumption, was taking it very slowly indeed.

"Are you sick, or lovesick, or what?" Geoff asked him on the second night when the beer in his glass descended at an unprecedentedly pedestrian rate.

"No, just taking it easy. So far this trip hasn't been as healthy as I expected and I wouldn't mind losing a few pounds."

"To please Laura?"

"Not really. She's not bothered about my weight, but I don't see the point of doing a long walk like today and then eating and drinking too much," he said, placing the roll of bread that he'd just grabbed back into the basket.

"I agree, but you must admit that meeting Laura has influenced you a bit," I said, hoping that my gentle prompting might be more effective in drawing him out than Geoff's less subtle attempts to persuade him to bare his soul regarding a liaison that none of us had expected, least of all him.

"Maybe, but she likes me just the way I am."

"She doesn't *know* you, Harry," said Geoff. "Until she's seen something of your rough edges you won't be sure that things are going to work out," he said with an encouraging smile.

"Geoff."

"Yes."

"Shut up."

"Right-ho." He raised his hands in surrender. "What shall we talk about then, seeing as the hot topic of conversation is out of bounds?"

"Tomorrow's trip," I said, unfolding the map.

"Yes, let's speed westwards and see if the Alpujarras have anything better to offer than this," said Geoff.

"Er, it's a pretty good place this," I said, pointing at the afterglow of the sunset. "Were you expecting something better? We're not in the Himalayas, after all."

"Oh, it's fine, but maybe we've seen all there is to see here and ought to press on."

"*I* don't want to rush away from this scenery," said Harry, pulling the map towards him. "We can follow this squiggly road west tomorrow and maybe pop up this one that seems to go right into the mountains. There's a village up there."

I prised his fat thumb off it. "Trevélez. Have you heard of it, Geoff?"

"Jamón."

"What?"

"Ham. Cured ham. That's what it's famous for," he said, looking proud of his knowledge, though recent studies (probably) show that 97% of Spaniards know that Trevélez is renowned for its cured ham.

"It's not too far, as the crow flies, but that road looks like it might be Bambi's hardest test yet," I said.

"I checked her oil again earlier. Not a drop less than a week ago. I certainly know how to choose a vehicle," Geoff said, proudly again, despite his fluky EBay find.

"I'll see if there's a campsite there," I said, as the Wi-Fi was excellent.

"What about our sense of advent–"

"Shush, Geoff," said Harry.

"Yes, there is one, and it looks fine. I have a feeling that it might be even better than this one."

12

My one regret about volunteering to drive was that I would have appreciated one of the best roads I've ever been along even more had I been a passenger, preferably up front. The thirty or so miles from Laroles to Trevélez are truly delightful and probably best appreciated by bike – if you're fit enough – as until the last northward stretch up to one of the highest villages in Spain – at 1486 metres – there was very little traffic. This was just as well, as the lack of a central white line on the narrow but well-surfaced road meant that I rounded each of the innumerable bends with great caution.

"We'd be there by now if I'd been driving," said Geoff from behind.

"Shut up and look out of your portholes," said Harry. "Who'd want to rush along a road like this?"

"Geoff would," I said.

"Always rushing and never arriving anywhere," Harry quipped.

"Ha, you'll see. I've just had an idea that'll make my fortune," he said, before lapsing into a silence intended to be pregnant, but which gave birth to no response from either of us.

After half a dozen more bends I felt it my duty to express interest.

"Tell us then."

"Nope, the pair of you clearly have the curiosity of a… a blind hamster, so I shall keep it to myself."

"Fair enough," said Harry.

"Tell us when you're ready. I think we're almost there."

The five or six white villages we'd already passed had all looked charming, but none could compare to the first view of Trevélez up ahead, on the other side of a sparsely wooded ravine; a view which got steadily better until our arrival provoked a sceptical remark from Geoff, despite his head having been thrust between ours for the last ten minutes.

"Touristville," he said on seeing the proliferation of restaurants, hotels, rural lodgings and ham shops, not to mention a handful of parked coaches.

"It does seem well-endowed for a village of eight hundred people," I had to admit.

"That's a good sign, and we're going to the campsite," said Harry.

To get there I followed the road round and began to drive down the other side of the ravine, before turning right into the site, parking, and watching my companions race over to the seemingly magnetic restaurant terrace. As the thirty miles had taken us a mere hour and a half it was still too early for lunch, so after imbibing a cold beer and the great view we decided to check in and set up camp.

"How about one of these cabins for a change?" I suggested after perusing a leaflet.

"Harry's snoring will keep me awake."

"I don't think I'll snore much here."

"How do you know?"

"Well, I think I snore more when I've drunk a good bit, and as I'm going to be taking it easy I doubt I'll snore."

"You might become a teetotaller eventually," I said.

"Don't be daft." He took the leaflet. "Hmm, let's splash out and get a big one, so we can have a proper bed each."

This we did, though it wasn't too dear, and after unpacking we decided to buy some bread from the shop and cook up a quick lunch. As Harry said, Bambi had been lugging all those cans of food through Spain for no apparent reason and it would be foolish to arrive at Gibraltar with most of our stores intact.

"They might increase the value of Bambi though," I said.

"No-one'll buy her," said Harry, shaking his head. "We've grown to like her, but let's face it, she's still a pig-ugly right-hand-drive van. We'll end up giving her away."

Geoff sniggered. Not any old snigger, to be followed by a droll or disparaging comment, but a snigger laden with a depth of meaning which he intended us to discover by using our wits; in other words, one of his guessing games.

"You got a sore throat?" Harry asked.

"Me? Not at all," he said, chortling this time, before looking at each of us in turn, twice.

"Who cares anyway? She didn't cost us much and we'll have had our money's worth by the end of the trip," I said, as unwilling to play the game as Harry was. He'd walked off to buy the bread and I began to search through the tins for something appealing.

"No, we might not need to worry about selling Bambi," Geoff said.

"How about minced beef and onions, with a tin of beans thrown in?"

"Whatever," he said, before stalking off to the cabin, which seemed pretty clean after the interior of Bambi, but I don't think more refined people would have been impressed by the dust in the corners and the single pubic hair in the shower. It was better than the shack back in Jarafuel, but by no means spotless and pretty shabby. When Harry arrived there about ten minutes later he was glowering.

"Was the bread expensive?" I asked.

He glowered a bit more, but mixed with the glower was a cunning expression not often seen on his round and relatively wrinkle-free face.

"You didn't lock Bambi's back door," he said to me.

"No, there's not much worth nicking."

"Someone's been in there."

"Yes, that'd be me. I've just brought those." I pointed to the tins which Geoff had emptied into a saucepan.

He looked down at my sandalled feet, so I looked too. They were a bit dusty, but otherwise unchanged. By now the glower had gone and a new expression had taken its place; a mixture of Sherlock Holmes, as played by Basil Rathbone, and a rugby player about to enter a scrum.

"Just checking your feet hadn't shrunk," he said with Geoff-like abstruseness.

"No, still nines, I think."

"The prints in the van were more like fours, maybe fives."

We both looked over at Geoff, but his feet hadn't shrunk either.

"So…"

"Yes, we've had a burglar," Harry said, raising his bushy eyebrows in a far from displeased way.

"Have they taken anything?"

"Not that I could see."

"Probably a kid, or kids."

"A single suspect, unless he or she had accomplices outside the van keeping watch. Maybe a young person, but possibly a woman, or a small-footed male," he said. In his formative years of policing Harry had considered switching to CID, but he'd found his potential colleagues so obnoxious and cynical that he'd decided against it. He said he would have missed the Saturday night fights in Morecambe too, but I think he'd sometimes regretted not becoming a sleuth.

"Have you locked it then?"

"Course not. I intend to find out who it is and apprehend him, or her, before handing them over to my Spanish colleagues."

"Haven't you retired?" Geoff asked, looking up from his stirring.

"You never lose the instinct. The door's unlocked and I've left my phone on one of the benches."

"Was that wise?"

"It's only a cheap one and I know Laura's number off by heart," he said, proving his great love for her as I've always found phone numbers with more than six digits impossible to memorise. "If they take it a felony will have been committed and I'll track them down, assuming they're on site." He rubbed his hands together and grinned.

After we'd eaten our tinned food on bread – for there was no toaster – the grin still flickered intermittently across his face.

"Who's up for a walk?" asked Geoff.

"Me, after a short rest."

"I'll be keeping watch this afternoon," said Harry.

"Don't be daft. We've got loads of paths to explore," I said, waving the little walking map I'd picked up in reception.

"Needs must."

"Besides, if they see you in Bambi they'll do a runner. If they don't nick anything I doubt the police will want to bother coming out here," said Geoff, now stretched out on his bed.

"Ah, but they won't see me."

"Are you going to watch from here, or somewhere else?" I asked, picturing him perched high up in a pine tree.

"Nope." He paused, but Geoff's latest conundrum was too recent for either of us to wish to quiz him. "I've cleared out the top bit over the cab and I'll hide there, under my sleeping bag."

"You won't fit," said Geoff.

"And if you do you'll suffocate," I said, as although almost all the campsite was shaded by trees it was still pushing thirty degrees. "I doubt they'll come now anyway. I reckon they've staked it out and will return after dark," I added, as it would have been a shame for him to miss the walk for so stupid a reason.

"Hmm, all right then. I'll lock her up for now."

"Why not just lock her up, full stop," said Geoff.

"If there's a thief about it's my duty to nab him, or her. If we all turned a blind eye there'd be bloody anarchy."

We did a relatively short walk that afternoon. After following a path to the village alongside a stream, Geoff urged us up through the tourism tainted streets at a rapid rate until we left the last houses behind. We then followed an assortment of tracks and paths which finally led us back to the campsite. While above the village we'd gazed up at the peak of Mulhacén, the highest mountain in Europe if you don't count the Alps and the Caucasus.

"I shall climb that tomorrow," said Geoff.

"I don't think so. There's a lot of snow up there and you haven't got the gear," I said, pointing to his well-worn walking shoes.

"I'll get as near as I can then."

"I suggest we all head up that way and see how it goes. Maybe we'll reach one of the little tarns, so we'll be able to refresh ourselves there and eat our lunch," I said, doubting we'd manage it as Harry was still far from being a mountain goat and I would stick with him. "And we'll buy a couple of small rucksacks when we pass through the village."

"I'd like that, and I hope to have resolved my case by then," said Harry as he changed into his swimming trunks. "I'll have my dinner early and take up my position before nightfall."

"Masochist," said Geoff.

"It's my vocation, something which you don't have."

"Or do I? I still haven't told you my plan."

"Tell us whenever you're ready, but it's time for a swim," I said, before we all went for a dip in the chilly pool.

While Geoff and I were drinking our pre-dinner beers, Harry was finishing his chicken and salad bocadillo, washed down by mineral water. He looked up at the darkening sky.

"Right, a quick coffee and I'm off to my hideaway."

"Do you plan to stay there all night?" I asked.

"I hope not. I'm bent double up there and it's not too comfy. If there's nothing doing by about midnight I'll crash out on one of the benches."

"Then they'll see you and run off. You won't even get a glimpse of them," said Geoff.

"Ah, but that's why I asked the nice waitress for this," he said, producing a thin bobbin of cotton thread. "I attach one end to the door handle and the other to my big toe. If they open it quick it'll snap, so I'll be up and on 'em like a shot. Yes, I think I've got every angle covered."

"Try not to use unnecessary force, Harry. They might end up arresting you instead of the evil intruder," I said.

"And try to get some sleep. We're attempting to scale Mulhacén tomorrow, remember," said Geoff, despite my having told him that three experienced English climbers had died up there about ten years previously, of hypothermia.

After eating some tasty lamb chops, among other things, we each ordered a whisky on the terrace and enjoyed the rapidly cooling evening air. Geoff zipped up his jacket and smiled at me, so I smiled back. After smiling back and forth for a while I decided that delaying the revelation of his great plan any longer would cause unnecessary stress, as with Harry's absurd surveillance and Geoff's quixotic walking ambitions I had enough to be going on with.

"Are you going to tell me about this plan of yours then?"

"Guess."

"No, just tell me."

"Well, the first point is that we won't be selling Bambi."

"Right, so you're going to keep her."

"Yes. I'll buy you chaps out, of course."

"We haven't paid you anything yet."

"That's true, so I suppose she's mine already."

"Yes, though you owe me for the boat ticket."

"Of course," he said, before sipping his drink and gazing at the twilit hills.

I realised it would be quicker and easier to humour him. "So you're going to drive back in her?"

"Ye-es."

"But not straight back."

"No."

"Through France?"

"Not exactly."

As the only way off the Iberian Peninsula is through France, I feared that his idea might be a really mad one.

"I know, you're going to drive down through Africa, and then…"

"No, that would be too ambitious; not for me, but for the van. I'm going to make my way back through Europe, maybe heading as far east as Hungary or Romania, and then go home and get down to the business end of things."

I guessed immediately what he planned to do. A lot of people do it nowadays, including me, though at the time I had no thoughts of writing a book about our little jaunt. At that point I'd been considering studying Spanish history when I got back and it was June who gave me the idea of writing this account. It has required some degree of patience and constancy, two qualities which Geoff has never been over-endowed with. The guitar, for instance, hadn't been touched for several days. Though I was almost certain of his money-making strategy – as if it were that easy – the whisky made me feel mischievous, so I resolved to tease the answer out of him.

"You're not going to take any people home with you, are you?"

"What do you mean?"

"Well, you know, get folk into Britain who fancy living there."

"What, people smuggling? Are you crazy?" he spluttered, literally, as he'd just taken a sip.

"It's just that you seem so sure that you're going to make your fortune. The only way to make a fortune quickly, as far as I know, is by doing something very bold, and probably illegal."

"No, it's nothing like that. It's a rational plan."

"Are you going to do some networking along the way? You know, make contacts and then set up some kind of business?"

"Like what?" he asked with a look of scepticism.

"Oh, I don't know… ah, you mentioned tourism. Are you going to attract people to the Lake District?"

"I think folk are already doing that, like tourist boards," he said gruffly, no longer enjoying the game.

"Drug smuggling?"

"What do you take me for?"

"Sorry, I just can't think of many ways of making a fortune by driving around Europe in a van."

"I'm going to write a *book* about it," he cried, before slumping back in his chair and puffing out his cheeks.

"Really? I'd never have thought of that. Have you done much writing?"

"Of course."

"Like what?"

"Like letters, well, emails and… stuff. I'm quite well-read, you know."

"Hmm, but you mainly read fantasy books. I suppose you could use your travel experiences and sort of… fantasise them," I said, thinking he'd be rather good at that.

"I won't need to. Once I set out on my own I'm sure all sorts of exciting things will happen to me. You two… well, I'm not saying you cramp my style, but I've always found that weird things tend to happen when I'm left to my own devices."

This was true, as whenever Harry and I met up with him he'd usually managed to get himself into one scrape or another, often involving women. I was sure that more unusual things would happen without our friendly buffer around him, but I thought I ought to warn him about the difficulty of his enterprise.

"I think it's a fine idea, Geoff, but it's not easy to make money by writing. Lots of people write books in these days of increased leisure, but it's not easy to find a publisher."

"But mine will be a unique adventure, in a unique vehicle."

"People travel everywhere these days. They ride around the world on bikes, they go and live in the rainforest for a couple of years, they trek across deserts and hang out with nomads. The world's becoming smaller all the time."

"Are you trying to put me off?"

"Not at all. I think it's a splendid idea, but do the trip first and keep your eyes open for other options. Besides, you haven't left Spain yet. Here you speak the language. Maybe you could run a few ideas past Laura when we get there."

"Hmm, I doubt she'll think of anything that I can't come up with myself."

As far as I knew he'd come up with zero ideas so far, but I didn't say so. Though his European trip was a nice plan, what he really needed was to earn some money or his aunt's inheritance would vanish before his eyes. I decided to ask Harry to have a word in Laura's ear when we got to her village. I could see Geoff staying in Spain and making a go of it, but hated to think of him being slaughtered by Rumanian bandits, if there are any. I'm a cautious type, as you can see, so any advice I give will rarely involve much risk.

"I wonder how Harry's getting on," I said.

Geoff's glum face lit up in an instant. "He'll be bored stiff, literally, but we can soon change that."

"Oh…"

"Another whisky, then we'll go and fulfil his vigilante dreams."

"Is that wise?"

"Look, he'll be bored to death in there and no-one else is going to break in. I bet it was some kids who just dared each other to get in the van."

"Let's have that whisky and think about it."

After another generous measure of Johnny Walker it seemed like an excellent idea, but I warned Geoff not to get too close to Harry's powerful, law-enforcing hands.

"I think it's just as well he retired, you know. His methods had become outdated. Even grabbing someone by the scruff of the neck could have got him into hot water. I reckon we should just open the door and stand well back," I said while we were waiting to pay.

"Oh, let's string it out a bit more, shall we?"

"How?"

"Well, it's only just after eleven, so he should still be huddled up above the cab. I think I'll creep in and see just how fast he can get down from there."

"He might be quicker than you think, and you don't want all that weight falling on you from a great height."

"Hmm, he will have gravity on his side, but it'll be all right. Are you ready?"

"Yes, what's my role?"

"Er, you could shuffle about outside, so he'll know there's more than one of us."

In the event I stood under a tree well back from the van, in order to run forward and tell Harry it was Geoff if he began to blindly pummel him. In the light of the almost full moon I saw Geoff open the back door very slowly, no doubt hoping to catch him asleep, and I held my breath when he disappeared inside. What seemed like quite a long time had elapsed – probably about half a minute – when a bulky figure hurtled past me and leapt into the van. I rushed after him and heard a quickly stifled cry, before bounding inside and tripping over a tangle of limbs between the benches.

"Harry, it's Geoff," I yelled from the top of the pile.

"I know, I can tell by the shape of his nose."

"Mm…mm…mm," uttered Geoff from the bottom of the pile.

"What?" asked Harry.

"Mm… mm… hand off my mouth, you great ape."

"Sorry, Geoff, I didn't know it was you, at first."

I rolled onto the left-hand bench and Harry pushed himself up and onto the other one, leaving a motionless Geoff on the floor.

"I hope you haven't crushed him to death," I said.

"No, I pounced like a leopard."

Geoff slowly pushed himself up onto his knees and began to giggle. "That's sobered me up. Bloody hell, Harry, hiding outside wasn't part of your plan."

"Well, I got so stiff up there that I thought I'd have a change."

"No real burglars then?" I asked.

"No, I heard a couple of kids outside a while ago, so I cleared my throat and they scarpered. I guess it was one of them who came inside earlier. Still, thanks to this pillock I got to put my plan into practice. I haven't lost my touch yet," he said, patting Geoff on the head. "Come on, I might as well sleep in the cabin."

After gazing up at the incredibly bright stars for a while, we trudged off to bed.

"Did I snore last night?" Harry asked the next morning.

"Not that I heard," I said.

"I don't know, I think I'm still concussed," said Geoff, looking like a talking corpse under the white sheet.

"It's after eight. We need to get a good breakfast inside us and set off up the mountain if we want to reach a tarn," I said, looking forward to our hike.

After eating our continental breakfast in the bar and buying some bocadillos to take with us, we walked by the stream to the village, where we transferred our plastic bags into two cheap knapsacks, purchased at a small supermarket. I think they were intended for younger people, judging by the cartoony graphics, and although they did the job, they hardly made us look like experienced mountaineers.

"I'd better not go up Mulhacén with one of these on my back," said Geoff as we plodded up through the village.

"No, maybe not. We'll go as far as we can without getting too tired, as coming down will be hard work too."

After over three hours' walking we reached a tarn called Laguna Hondera, which I thought quite an achievement, especially for Harry, who though slow had hardly stopped to rest at all. At that height – about 2700 metres, I later found – there was hardly any vegetation, apart from around the tarn itself, and the snowline began not far above us. The scenery, needless to say, was spectacular and well worth the effort, which made me think it a pity that so many tourists arrive in Trevélez, wander around a bit, buy a leg of ham or some souvenirs, and climb back into the coach. Even a relatively short walk beyond the village would make the trip so much more worthwhile.

Despite the sunshine the air was decidedly chilly and a bit thinner than down below, so after washing our sweaty faces we decided to head part of the way down before eating. I think the point we reached was where the real climbing began, but those final seven hundred metres to the top of Mulhacén would have been too far even for Geoff. In midsummer, with better boots and clothing, and less infantile rucksacks, any fit, experienced walker should be able to reach the summit and descend in a day, but we were quite content with our modest feat and the glimmering water of the tarn has stuck in my mind to this day.

We reached base camp at about five and collapsed onto our beds for a well-earned siesta, before eating a gargantuan dinner at the restaurant and deciding to stay for another day. The next morning, all feeling our age for once, we strolled up a track to join the GR7 walking route, which stretches from somewhere in France to Tarifa, the southernmost point of Europe. Geoff wanted us to walk down to Busquístar, about eight miles away, and hitch a lift back, but Harry and I baulked at this suggestion.

"We might struggle to get a lift, all three of us," I said.

"Grown men don't hitchhike," said Harry.

"Chickens," said Geoff.

"You go ahead," I said. "Quite a lot of cars go up to Trevélez on that road."

"Yes, it'll be good practice for your transcontinental adventure," said Harry, who had been apprised of Geoff's plan the previous day.

"I will then. If I haven't returned by nightfall you could drive down the road and look for me."

"We could," said Harry.

"You're bound to get a lift," I said as we turned round and headed back up the picturesque path.

Over lunch in the restaurant I asked Harry if he thought Laura might have any ideas as to how Geoff could earn a living in Spain.

"I can ask. She seems to know a lot of people, so she might know someone who needs someone."

"Someone like Geoff?"

"Who knows? I reckon he's a good grafter when he likes what he's doing. I'll tell her that."

"I'm glad I've retired," I said, pushing my empty plate away.

"Me too. I liked work, but I like this better."

Geoff arrived back safe and sound just as we were undressing for our siestas, something which would have been decidedly uncomfortable in Bambi, due to her great ability to absorb the heat of the sun.

"A Scottish chap who gave me a lift has given me an idea," he said, sounding chirpier than I would have liked at that moment in time.

"Can you tell us later?" I said, before yawning loudly.

"I'll tell you now, so your subconscious can process it while you sleep," he said, being far fonder of subliminal brainwork than actively thinking things through.

"Make it quick," said a horizontal Harry.

"Transport."

"That's a wide area of endeavour," I said.

"Well, the Scottish chap does airport runs, unofficially, and he also has a big van to do removals, mainly from one part of Andalucia to another, but he has done the odd trip back to Britain, unofficially."

"Unofficially?"

"Well, he hasn't got a taxi or a business. He just does people favours, for money. He came here to pick up some Brits and drive them to Malaga airport. A hundred euros. Easy-peasy."

"Minus fuel, and where does he live?" I asked.

"Oh, somewhere west of Malaga. Some tourist hellhole, no doubt."

"I imagine a lot of people do what he's doing. It won't be easy to make a living, and certainly not in Bambi."

"Why not? Bambi's perfect. She's so versatile, you see. She's a van and can also carry people." He raised his hands and smiled.

"She's not a proper van because there's no loading door and only two people can ride in her, officially," said Harry in the monotonous voice of one who is eager to sleep.

"Hmm, that's a point. Still, what do you think of the general idea?"

"Transport," I said, stifling a real yawn. "I shall repeat that word to myself as I fall asleep and tell you if the old grey matter comes up with anything when I wake up. OK?"

"Fair enough. Shall I wake you in an hour?"

"And a half," I said, turning to face the wall.

I awoke to find Geoff's face about a foot from mine.

"Anything?" he asked.

"Any what?"

"Transport ideas."

"Nothing yet. I might need a full night's sleep to fully process the idea."

Harry's bed creaked as he turned over to face us. "I've had a dream," he muttered.

"About a better, fairer world?" I asked.

"No, but Geoff was in it. He was talking Spanish… in Spain, I think." He sat up and stretched. "Is that any use?"

"Not much."

"It might be," I said. "I think if you want to work in Spain you'll have to come and live here. I don't think you'd get a job from England and what the Scottish chap does sort of points the way. You come and live here, cheaply, make friends with people, then maybe you can use your languages skills and… other skills to make some money. How does that sound?"

"Interesting. Yes, I was thinking along the same lines while you were both asleep."

"Bullshit," said Harry.

"I *was*, but Jeremy's sort of clarified it. Maybe I'll just stay here when you've gone."

I sat bolt upright. "No, no, no. First you go home and sort out your affairs there. I'm not emptying your flat and getting quizzed by the landlord."

"It's furnished."

"I don't care. I can spare a couple of cubic metres of garage space, but you'll put your stuff there yourself. Is that clear?"

"All right, Mr Teacher."

"Besides, I'll probably be doing the same as you pretty soon," said Harry, now fully dressed in old shorts and a baseball vest.

"That's true, but you'll be coming to live with Laura," Geoff said, nodding several times.

Harry's face clouded. "*I* will, yes. You'd better get on the right side of her when we go there. She might know someone who'll rent you a room, someone other than herself."

I clapped. "All food for thought. Now let's have a swim before we get some real food."

"Then off to Laura's tomorrow," said Geoff, slapping his thighs.

"Nope. There's still a lot of Alpujarras left and we're not rushing off yet," said Harry.

"I doubt we'll beat this place," said Geoff.

"We'll find out tomorrow."

13

As I said, the road up to Trevélez shoots off north into the mountains, so when we set off the next morning we headed towards another road that penetrates the sierra. To get there we trundled down the road to the west of the ravine that we'd come up and drove past Busquístar, Pórtugos and Pitres, before beginning to climb another long hill into the mountains. The scenery had been great all the way, but the point on the road where you first see three villages at once – Pampaneira, Bubión and Capileira – each one perched higher up a wooded gorge, is truly breathtaking, especially when the mist still lingers over the white houses as it did that morning.

"This is even better than Trevélez," I said.

"Let's head up to the highest one," said Harry.

"It'll be another touristville, you'll see," said Geoff.

"It doesn't matter if there's a campsite," said Harry.

Although Capileira certainly caters for the holidaymaker and quite a lot of new building has been done to the north of the original village, it didn't seem quite as commercial as Trevélez, which I believe has been a tourist destination for many more years. Eateries abound in Capileira and, despite having been in Granada province for several days, we finally realised that when you order a beer or a glass of wine you usually get a free tapa. Harry was delighted to discover this seemingly altruistic tendency, so instead of the single beer we'd planned to drink, we ended up having four, each in a different bar, just to make sure, Harry asserted, that it hadn't been a one-off.

"That's four out of four so far," I said as we munched slices of blood sausage on bread which reminded me of Burgos. "We'd better find out where we're staying before we continue this experiment."

"The beer's making me hungrier and the tapas are making me thirstier," said Harry.

"I think that's the idea. We'll be legless before we're full," I said, before asking the young waiter about campsites.

"The campsite is now run by the village," he said. "Before it was very bad, so the municipality took it over."

"Is it better now?"

"No, it is worse, but now it is free. You must take toilet paper and the showers are cold, but it is a good place to camp and not busy right now."

"And free, like the tapas," said a rosy-faced Harry.

The slim, bronzed young man scrutinised the jolly giant, before disappearing into the kitchen and returning with a big plate of patatas bravas.

"Eat this too, on me. You British get too enthusiastic about our free tapas."

I complimented him on his English and he told us he'd studied it at school, before learning to use it by talking to customers. After paying and promising to return later, we jumped back into Bambi and followed his directions to the self-service campsite, just outside the village to the north-east. The setup was pretty similar to the facilities provided near Castell de Castells, except there were showers too, and I thought it a shrewd idea of the village council to take it over, as the campers would undoubtedly spend some money in the village, if only in the shops. There were four tents and a VW camper van when we arrived, though bits of litter suggested that it had been fuller the night before, a Saturday.

"It's just a week since we were at a place very much like this," I said as I watched Harry erect his tent with masterly skill.

"It feels like an age," he said, resting his rubber mallet on his knee and gazing down the mountainside, no doubt thinking of Laura. It really was unselfish of him not to want to rush into her arms as soon as possible, and I reflected that Geoff could learn a lot from him, though it's hard to teach a middle-aged dog new tricks. After a night or two there I would propose driving straight to Laura's village, as he must be longing to see her, and Geoff wouldn't object as he had his own motives for getting there and ingratiating himself.

"I expect you're dying to see Laura," Geoff said some time later, after we'd eaten another three-can combination: spaghetti hoops, beans and meatballs this time with, rather than on, bread.

"I'm looking forward to it, yes." He licked his lips. "I enjoyed that."

"I know I would be. Ha, whenever I'm with a woman I'm pretty insatiable," he said with a slitty-eyed leer.

"Laura isn't one of your floozies though," I said lightly, sensing that Harry had no desire to allude to, let alone discuss, his future sex life.

"I haven't *just* been out with floozies, as you so archaically call them. With Carmela, Andrea and... er, Sarah I came very close to matrimony."

"Sarah from Garstang?" I asked.

"Yes."

"But didn't she emigrate to New Zealand shortly after you split up?"

"Yes, she was heartbroken, poor girl. If she hadn't been so clinging we might have made a go of it, but in the end I had to chuck her and I think she just needed to get as far away from me as possible. I hope your Laura doesn't prove to be as clinging as some of my women, Harry."

"She can be as clinging as she likes. Couples tend to cling, if they love each other," he said, surprising us both by the use of that four-letter word.

"Shall we head that way tomorrow?" I asked.

"No, we've got to explore around here first. I wouldn't mind going the day after though, just for a couple of nights, then we'll carry on."

"How long have you got left, Jeremy?" Geoff asked, reminding me of my thirty-day limit which June had been unclingy enough not to refer to in her numerous texts and our two short conversations.

I looked at the date on my watch. "Er, I reckon I've got ten or eleven days left, but that's not set in stone. She's in Croatia right now on a yoga retreat, so she's feeling pretty laid back."

"I've heard some dodgy stories about those yoga retreats," said Geoff, another leer heralding more sexual innuendo, one of his specialities. "They can turn into fully-fledged orgies if the chemistry's right."

"That's all right. June and I have had an open relationship for many years now."

"Really? I've always wanted to have one of those."

"Yes, we're very open with each other. I'm sure she'll tell me if she has it away with her guru. Oh, that reminds me. I must remember to email Marta soon. Maybe I'll invite her over to stay when the season's over. You remember Marta, don't you? From the campsite in Cantabria."

"Hmm, vaguely. What are we doing this afternoon?"

"Walking, I guess."

"We always walk. Is there nothing else we can do?"

"We tried kayaking, but you didn't like that," said Harry.

"Only because of my hangover."

"You can't beat walking though," I said. "If you think about it, a lot of the best things in life are free, or cheap. Walking, reading…"

"And camping, here at least," said Harry. "Unless they're hiring hang gliders in the village, walking will suit me just fine, but not a long one this aft."

So it was that after allowing our wholesome meal to digest and the sun to cool we set off on an impromptu walk and ended up heading south-east on a track which climbed steadily along the side of the valley, giving us great views of all three villages. On the way back the towering peaks of the Sierra Nevada looked both ominous and appealing and I remembered something a teaching colleague had once told me.

"I think there's a road to Granada from here that goes right over the top of the mountain. A chap at school once cycled up it, many years ago. Shame we don't have bikes," I said, relieved that we didn't.

"We could hire some and have a potter up tomorrow," said Geoff as we entered the village streets. "It's not that far on a bike. I bet we could do it in a couple of hours, then it's downhill all the way back."

"I like the downhill bit, but I doubt that anyone'll rent out bikes in a place this small," said Harry, presumably as pleased as I was that the proposal was purely hypothetical.

"Let's call in at that bar with the friendly chap and ask him," Geoff said, forging ahead up the street.

"Uh-oh," I said to Harry.

"Don't worry, there'll be no bikes. Tomorrow we'll walk part of the way up the road. Hey, maybe someone'll give us a lift to the top, then we can just walk down."

"That'd suit me. I'm good at walking downhill."

"Your friend he speaks good Spanish," said the friendly chap when we arrived to find Geoff already quizzing him hard. "The road to Veleta is now closed to cars, but it is still possible to cycle up there." He looked us up and down, especially Harry. "It is about thirty kilometres though, and very hard work, especially the first part. Do you cycle a lot?"

"Nope," said Harry.

"No," said I.

"I do, but with all the gears that bikes have these days it'll be pretty easy if we take our time," said Geoff.

"Oh, I'd definitely be up for it," I enthused, "but I doubt that–"

"Juan Antonio's just told me that there's a place down the road in Bubión that hires bikes; run by an English couple, he thinks."

"Ah, right. The trouble is, Geoff, that me and Harry haven't cycled since we were kids…"

"No problem. You take it nice and easy and sooner or later you'll get to the top. I'll shoot up ahead of you to see what it's like, then whizz down and see you up."

"I'm up for it," said that unsuspecting fool Harry. "I'm not that bothered if I don't get to the top, but I'll have a go."

"Well, I guess I will too then."

"Great. After we've had coffee I'll drive down in Bambi and pick up the bikes, then we can make a really early start, as I think it might be a tad warm again tomorrow," Geoff said.

Yes, it is better that you start at seven o'clock or before, and take a lot of water and some food," said Juan Antonio, smiling and nodding.

"Have you ever cycled up?" I asked him.

"One time, yes, when I was younger and braver than now."

Considering that he can't have been much over thirty and looked as fit as a fiddle, I deduced that we'd let ourselves in for something of an ordeal.

So it was that shortly after sunrise the next day we mounted our flashy mountain bikes, each carrying two large water bottles, while Geoff volunteered to carry the sturdier of our two childish rucksacks, laden mostly with liquids as, he said, we would just zoom down the hill and go straight to the bar for lunch and report back to the politely sceptical Juan Antonio. The evening before we'd all eaten big steaks with rice at a restaurant on the main street – because Geoff had said that Tour de France racers ate nothing else when they were on the job – and turned in early to get plenty of rest.

We followed the road straight from the campsite, zigzagging up through tall pine trees, and I must say that I found the first ten or fifteen minutes enjoyable. It was a cool, crisp morning and after engaging bottom gear, as Geoff had instructed, it was pretty easy to keep the pedals turning without getting out of breath. I felt I could go much faster, but didn't wish to demoralise Harry, who was plodding along contentedly at my side. After setting our sensible speed, Geoff had forged ahead to warm his legs up, he said, and the way he swung the bike from side to side belied the fact that he hadn't cycled at all for a couple of months. After a while the tarmac petered out and on the dusty track my back wheel slipped from time to time when I thrust the pedals down too hard, but this proved to be a short-lived problem, as quite soon my thighs began to burn and it no longer felt like such a doddle.

"How far did he say it was to the top?" Harry asked, already panting.

"About thirty kilometres, so less than twenty miles."

"That's almost as far as going from Lancaster to Kendal."

"Yes, except all uphill."

"I think I'll walk for a bit," said my wise friend.

"Me too."

Walking was a relief after cycling, then cycling was OK again after a respite, as the gradient wasn't too steep and we were taking our time. After about an hour, however, we decided to have a ten minute rest, judging that we'd covered about a quarter of the way, as we didn't count the return journey because anyone can ride a bike downhill. While sitting on some rocks by the side of the track we heard juddering and skidding sounds, before Geoff appeared round the bend, bringing a cloud of dust with him.

"Tired already?" he asked, looking sweaty but full of beans.

"We're pacing ourselves. Ten minutes rest every hour," I said, ready to get going again.

"OK, I'll ride along with you for a while."

On remounting, the spongy saddle didn't feel as comfy as before and my legs protested vehemently at the resumption of this unfamiliar exercise.

"Bloody hell, my arse is sore," said Harry, voicing my own thoughts.

"Stand up on the pedals for a bit like this," said Geoff.

I stood up, my back wheel slipped, and I sat down again. "Ouch, I think I'll walk for a bit," I said, before Harry and I dismounted simultaneously.

"I can't *walk*. It's against my principles," said Geoff, wobbling along beside us. "I'll push on for a while."

Left to our own devices our spells of walking gradually outweighed our cycling stints, until it got to the point where we just didn't feel like getting our legs over anymore.

"Better save the skins of our arses for the downhill bit," Harry said.

"Yes, it's pretty clear that we're not going to get to the top, so let's just take it easy. The next time Eddy Merckx comes back we'll tell him to press on alone."

When he came back he expressed dismay at our paltry efforts and, after unloading our bocadillos, set off for his definitive assault on the summit. It was with far less swagger that he resumed his ascent, however, and I reflected that it had been pretty dumb of him to waste energy by riding up and down. I'm not certain, but I think Harry and I got about half way to the top before declaring ourselves satisfied with our manly effort and flopping down to eat the sandwiches that we'd saved for the high point of our journey. After lolling around for half an hour the sun was burning down and, as the sweat must have washed away our sun cream by then, I suggested heading back down to the campsite.

"Let's coast back down," were my exact words, but coast wasn't the word I would have employed a few minutes later as the vibrations of the bike pummelled my backside and my arms began to go numb. I don't mind admitting that we rested twice more on the way down, but we got back in one piece and both headed off for our well-earned cold showers.

"I feel like I could have gone a bit further now," said Harry a while later, beer in hand.

"Yes, but we'd never have made it to the top, so it doesn't matter. I enjoyed it, in a way," I said, indelicately rubbing the sore skin between my legs. "But I don't think cycling's for me."

"Do you think Geoff'll make it to the top?"

I pondered for a while. After considering his sprightly start, the unnecessary distance he'd covered, and the unmistakable signs of tiredness that he'd shown on disappearing up the track for the last time, I concluded that he wouldn't.

"Or if he does, he'll have to walk quite a bit, so he'll be absolutely ages."

"He'll say he made it even if he didn't," said Harry.

"Hmm, probably. Let's see how long he takes before we pass judgement."

About an hour later Geoff sped into camp, skidded to a halt like I used to do on my Raleigh Chopper, leant the bike against Bambi, and beamed at us like a man about to tell a barefaced lie.

"That wasn't too bad," he said, his new nose looking dangerously red.

"Is it a good view from the top?" I asked, for there was no need to ask the million dollar question.

"Spectacular. You can see for miles around."

"Obviously," said Harry. "What could you see?"

"Oh, the peak of Mulhacén just a bit higher up, all the Alpujarras, the Med, and Granada in the valley to the north."

The fact that Granada lay to the north-west was a excusable error, so I casually asked him if he'd been able to see the Alhambra.

"Er, yes. Are there any cold beers left?"

"A couple," Harry said.

While he retrieved a can of beer Harry and I conferred.

"Let's go to Juan Antonio's bar for dinner, shall we?" I suggested a while later, after we'd loaded the bikes into Bambi.

Geoff frowned. "Why not try somewhere new?"

"Oh, he'll be dying to know how we got on," said Harry, his hands on his lap, though I knew that mentally he was rubbing them together.

No doubt you'll have guessed the next bit, so I'll spare you the gory details, and some of Geoff's blushes, as the mendacious muppet will probably read this too. After several beers and tapas at Juan Antonio's bar – for he proved to be the owner – our cooperative host began to quiz Geoff regarding the features of his route. Had he passed a tarn while cycling in the shadow of Mulhacén? Had the road flattened out after that point? Was there much snow on the final, dead-end track to the summit of Veleta? Had he been able to make out the coast of Africa?

If we'd seated him in the Mastermind chair his discomfiture couldn't have been greater as he stuttered out his replies, and Juan Antonio remained admirably poker-faced as he delivered his killer blow.

"Did you like the three little lakes you can see just below the summit, Geoff?"

"Oh, yes, they were wonderful. Such clear, blue water," he replied with aplomb, relieved by the direct question.

"Oh… wait, sorry, no. I was thinking of Mulhacén. From Veleta there is only one lake nearby, I now recall," he said, before busying himself behind the bar.

Geoff's glowing face went redder still and when he tipped back his head to take a drink he found four brown eyes boring into his sheepish blue ones.

"Could you make out the church tower the Christians plonked down in the Alhambra?" I asked, despite that fabulous Moorish palace being at least twenty miles from the peak and, Juan Antonio thought, barely discernible from there.

"All right, all right! Perhaps I didn't make it quite to the top," he cried, slamming down his glass.

"Perhaps?" Harry asked.

"Quite?" I asked.

"Well I got further than you two, and I wasn't *that* far from the top, but I haven't been out on the bike for ages and my legs just went."

"Where did they go?" asked Harry.

Seeing his profound embarrassment, I asked him why he hadn't taken his time and walked some of the way.

"I told you, walking's against my principles when I'm cycling. If I'd walked it wouldn't have counted."

"But you'd have got there," I said.

"And been able to tell us what the view was like," said Harry.

"Oh, it just seemed simpler to tell you I'd made it. I didn't want to disappoint you."

"But you *have* disappointed us, Geoff," said Harry, clearly feeling less benevolent than myself. "We'll never know when to believe you from now on."

"Oh, come on! People tell tall tales when they do sport. It's part of the… sport."

Harry relented, a bit. "All right then, we'll let you off this time. I shan't tell Laura either. I don't want her to think I hang out with liars."

"And thanks for getting the bikes and taking them back," I said. "How much do we owe you?"

"Nothing, it's on me." He looked at Harry. "So you won't tell Laura then?"

"No, but it's no big deal."

"No, but maybe Belgians take a dim view of fibbing and I want to make a good impression, in case she can… help me out," he said, struggling to get the last few words out.

Harry patted him on the back. "Don't worry. Tomorrow all this will be forgotten. Now, I'm still hungry, so I'd better order another beer."

14

On the three hour trip to Laura's village we made no reference to Geoff's deceitfulness, but he was subdued for most of the journey, preferring to hide his shame in the back of Bambi. On the whole I thought a contrite, diffident Geoff was better than a brash and boastful one, given the importance of his first visit to his future friend-in-law's house. His transport idea was all very well, but what he needed was to make contacts and this was the only opportunity he would have, as folk don't tend to take three men travelling in a laughable, pint-sized camper van very seriously. The only time he spoke up during the entire journey was when Harry suggested stopping for coffee in the small town of Órgiva after completing our scenic but torturous descent from Capiliera.

"I don't mind," he muttered.

"Have you been looking out of your portholes?"

"No." He leant forward between us and spotted a couple of the hippy-like people who peppered the main street along with sundry standard foreigners and a few locals. "Good grief, what's happened to her?" he exclaimed on seeing an elderly woman dressed in a tie-dyed smock with what appeared to be a pink bird's nest on her head.

"She became old. Quite a few aging hippies live here, I believe, but if we stick around we might meet some younger ones too," I said.

"Like the ones you met back in Almeria," said Harry, right on cue.

"Drive on, drive on, for the love of God."

"There might be a few in Laura's village," Harry said.

"Then I'll hitchhike to the coast and wait for you there."

So we had our coffee in Lanjarón, a thriving spa town often referred to as the gateway to the Alpujarras, before ruling out an ambitious cross-country route that I'd advocated and heading down the dual-carriageway to the coast, where Bambi reached her top speed of the whole trip – 59mph – before I brought her to heel lest we end up in the sea. After bypassing Motril we headed along the coastal motorway as far as Torrox, from where Bambi began yet another humungous ascent. On the twelve-mile climb I don't think there was a straight bit longer than a hundred yards and by the time we reached the striking white village of Cómpeta a formidable queue had formed behind us, including a tractor, though it was one of those powerful modern ones. The scenery had been quite pleasant, though less wooded than the Alpujarras, and the large number of houses dotted about on the hillside suggested that foreigners abounded in these parts, a suspicion confirmed when we reached our destination of Canillas de Albaida, a white village with more than its fair share of mature purple beings from the north of Europe, like ourselves.

After I'd pulled over on a tree-lined avenue with views of the village and the high mountains behind it, Harry jumped out and scuttled away to call Laura on his mobile.

"Why didn't he ring her from here?" asked Geoff.

"Because he won't want us to hear the sweet nothings he'll be whispering to her."

"She'd better not whisper back or he'll not hear a thing."

"She knows about his slight deafness."

"Can she lip-read in half a dozen languages too?"

"Probably. Let's leave them to it when we get there, shall we? We could go off for a beer or something."

"If he's anything like me he'll be banging away like a rabbit twenty minutes from now."

"And we'll be having a beer. Here he comes."

"She's going to nip down in the car, so just follow us," Harry said through the window.

Laura's Mini soon appeared and Harry got in before she had time to get out to greet us, which set the tone for most of our visit, as Harry was clearly determined to maximise his time alone with her. She led us up around the village to her large house near the top, where she hopped out and opened a garage door. She was about to usher us into it when she realised that Bambi's lofty height wouldn't fit, so she pointed to the widest part of the narrow street, before driving her car into the garage.

"Maybe she's a bit scatty," said Geoff.

"Not really. Bambi looks small, especially from the front. You only appreciate her towering bulk when you get up close," I said, before ushering him out so that I could park close to the wall.

Laura and Harry took their time coming out of the garage, so I guessed they'd been renewing their brief acquaintance with a few hugs and kisses, though in our presence they only ever showed their mutual affection with a little handholding and arm-stroking. Nor did they shoo us away and rush off to the bedroom, as after she had showed Geoff and I to our neat rooms, we were soon sitting on the patio overlooking a small pool, most of the village, and the green hills away towards the coast.

"Now tell me, what have you done since I last saw you?" she asked us as we tucked into a light lunch that she'd prepared earlier.

Harry looked at me, so I gave her a brief account of our stays in Laroles, Trevélez and Capileira, concluding with a brief mention of our cycle ride of the previous day.

"How nice! Some people go mountain biking around here, but most prefer walking, like me. So did you get to the top of Veleta?"

Geoff shot a scared glance at Harry, who began to tell the tale of our ride in tremendously pedantic detail, which was most unlike him. He told her how the idea was conceived, before explaining how we'd located the bike rental shop, and even told her what we'd eaten the night before and how he'd slept. By the time he got onto the ride itself, beads of sweat were rolling down Geoff's right temple – and presumably the left, but I couldn't see that – and he gave a lengthy description of how it had felt to mount a bike after so many years. His first ten minutes up the mountain took as many minutes to describe, by which time Geoff's beer glass was empty and he was looking at his tormentor like one imagines rabbits gaze into headlights.

Harry cleared his throat and glanced at Geoff. "Anyway, to cut a long story short, we got about two-thirds of the way up and decided to call it a day."

"Very sensible, I think, as none of you were prepared for it" said Laura. "I think you did very well to get so far."

"I was suited with that," said Harry.

"It was far enough for me," said I.

"Can I use the bathroom, please, Laura," said Geoff, looking pale under his tan, which sounds improbable, but without blood behind it, tanned skin tends to lose its glow.

After his little fright Geoff soon loosened up and we had a couple more beers and an interesting chat. It turned out that Laura's husband had been twelve years older than her and high up in the diplomatic service. After he'd succumbed to a grave illness she neither wished nor needed to continue working, so she'd sold up in Belgium and moved south. She liked the village and had settled in well, as the locals appreciated the fact that she could speak their language, but she often drove down to the coast where she had several Belgian friends.

"Are any of them in business? Geoff wants to come back to Spain, so he'll be looking for a job," said Harry with his old directness.

"Let me see," she said, though I was pretty sure the subject had been mentioned before. "Emilie still does some work as a dressmaker in Vélez-Málaga, but I don't suppose you could do that."

"I can sew buttons on," Geoff said, looking like an eager interviewee.

"Then there's Hugo. Yes, Hugo has his fingers in many cakes."

"Pies," Harry corrected.

"Sorry, in many pies. English isn't one of my stronger languages, but I'm sure you will change that, Harry dear."

"You'll soon be talking like a true northerner. So who's this Hugo?"

"He's an entrepreneur. He exports products from here to Belgium and vice versa. He's in his sixties now, but has no wish to retire."

"Does he export wine and olive oil?" Geoff asked.

"Hmm, maybe wine, but I know he sells a lot of vehicles. I think second-hand cars are cheaper in Belgium, so he buys them and brings them here. He doesn't often talk about his business when we meet, but you ought to see him."

"Transport," Geoff murmured. "Where does he live, Laura?"

"Near Torre del Mar, on the coast. He has a big house and an enormous garage which I've never seen inside. He drives smart cars, always different, so yes, I think vehicles are a big part of his business. I'll give him a call."

After a rapid French conversation she switched off her mobile and smiled at Geoff. "Can you go down to see him tomorrow morning? He's keen to meet you, but hasn't the time to come all the way up here."

"Of course," Geoff said, his broad smile slowly turning into a pensive frown. "I hope he doesn't think I'm a loony when he sees me in Bambi."

"Oh, you can't drive that… van all the way there and back. You must go in the Mini. We can set the satnav so you will reach his house easily."

"That's very kind of you, Laura. I'll take good care of your lovely car."

"Ha, that is something that Hugo might wish you to do. Would you mind driving BMWs and Mercedes from Belgium to Spain?"

"No, I wouldn't mind that at all," he positively gushed.

"I'll come with you tomorrow," I said, seeing the opportunity to give the courting couple some time alone. "You can drop me in town and pick me up afterwards."

Laura stood up. "That's settled then. Now, make yourselves at home. Have another beer, a swim or a siesta, and we'll have dinner in the village later."

"I bet they're at it now," said Geoff from his li-lo as I swam leisurely up and down the pool.

"Good for them. This Hugo chap sounds interesting."

"Yes, I'd prefer to work for myself, but I suppose I'd better learn the ropes first," said the man who had never been self-employed in his life.

"Just make sure if he offers you something that it's enough to live on and rent a place."

"Yes, though it'd put the kibosh on my European tour."

"You need to make money, Geoff, not spend it."

"True. We'll see what he says tomorrow."

I suppose our arrival at Laura's spelt the beginning of the end of our shared adventure, as following Geoff's visit to Hugo, both he and Harry had longer-term plans to think about. Don't worry, or heave a sigh of relief, as I'm not going to wind things up prematurely, but from now on our minds, if not our bodies, would be in different places. I was beginning to miss my wife too, and though I was looking forward to the last leg of our journey, I was also keen to see her again.

After whiling away a few hours in the pleasant seaside town of Torre del Mar, which though awash with foreigners still had a very Spanish feel to it, Geoff rolled up to the seafront café where we'd agreed to meet and swaggered over from the car with the look of a man who was set up for life. After spinning the key around his finger a few times, he looked around with a proprietorial air, before slipping into the chair opposite me.

"I suppose I could live here, if I have to," he said, screwing up his nose on hearing a tableful of Brits nearby.

"Does that mean you have a job?"

"I think so. Hugo's a perceptive old chap and immediately recognised my potential. I'm not sure that everything he does is entirely above-board, but the car import business sounds legal enough. He wants me to drive cars down. I'll normally fly there, but occasionally there's a Belgian who wants a car driving back," he said, before describing the lean, tanned, chain-smoker with a roguish twinkle in his eyes and an undying love of wheeling and dealing.

"I hope you don't get mixed up in anything dodgy, Geoff," I said, imagining a plaintive plea for help from a Spanish prison.

"No, I've told him that I want to stay on the right side of the law, and he assured me I would."

"What happened to the other guy?"

"What other guy?"

"Well, someone must have been doing the driving before you."

"Oh, I think he's just got more work on now, and he's fed up of driving himself."

"How much will he pay you?"

"A thousand a month, plus commission."

"Well, a thousand should be enough to get by on, but you might have to share a flat."

"Oh no, I'll triple or quadruple that with the commissions I'll get for flogging the cars. The grand's just a sort of retainer, in case things get slow."

"When do you start?"

"Well, I *could* start right away, but…"

"You have to sort out your affairs first," I firmly interposed.

"Yes, so I guess the sooner I get back, the sooner I can do that."

"A week either way won't make any difference. It's still quite a way to Gibraltar and we've more places to see."

"We *could* fly back from Malaga, of course."

Sensing mutiny in the air I decided that we ought to consult with Harry. He would cast the deciding vote and if he couldn't live without Laura, I feared that the route through Ronda I'd been planning might have to be aborted.

Still, I could always come back with June, I thought as Geoff piloted us swiftly back up into the sierra, but Harry gave short shrift to Geoff's pleas for a speedy return.

"Bollocks, we've come this far and we're not cutting it short now."

"Bollocks. That's a new word for me," said Laura from her wicker chair on the patio.

"You might learn a few more from Harry," I said. "What have you been up to today?"

"We've been walking, up there," Harry said, pointing north. "There are some great trails through the woods and I reckon we should do a long walk tomorrow, before heading off." He turned to Geoff. "To Gibraltar."

"Suits me," I said.

"I hope Hugo won't change his mind," Geoff said sulkily.

"Hugo is a man of his word," said Laura. "He would like you to start within a month, but there's no great rush."

"Have you spoken to him?"

"Yes, he called me. He thinks you're just the man for the job and has high hopes for you."

"I like him too. It's good to meet a man who recognises talent once in a while."

I shall say no more about Geoff's work prospects – though he did tell us about some of the more risqué facets of Hugo's business empire – not because I don't want to or can't be bothered, but because at the time of writing Geoff still harbours his own literary aspirations and has requested me to limit my efforts to the trip itself. If an actual book will ever emerge from that closet genius's busy brain I very much doubt, but a promise is a promise, so not another word about the Hugo-Geoff mercantile alliance.

The following morning we set off early and Laura led us round a lovely seven-mile loop on the mountain trails to the north and west of the village. We crossed and recrossed streams, plunged into dense pine and chestnut woods, scaled and descended steep paths, tramped through thickets of oleander bushes, ate our picnic lunch on a curious circular threshing floor, saw several majestic birds of prey, and all had a thoroughly good time. Laura was slightly fitter than Harry, which pleased him rather than otherwise, as he swore that when he came to live here he'd walk every day.

"So do you think you'll come here, rather than Laura going to Lancaster?" I asked him later by the pool.

"What do you think?" he said with a grin. "She'll come over about a fortnight from now and I'll take her up the Lakes, which she'll love, but after that I'll come here for the rest of the summer. If all goes well I guess I'll end up here permanently, so you and June will have to come out on holiday."

"Definitely. In spring or autumn, I reckon, as it's getting a bit hot now."

"This autumn then."

"I guess you'll be seeing quite a bit of Geoff too."

"Hmm, but it's a fair old trek up that road from the coast, so hopefully it won't be too often."

"You'd better keep an eye on him though."

"Oh, I will. I've told Laura I want to meet this Hugo bloke. If he's a con artist I'll know, as I've met enough over the years, but if Laura says he's all right, he must be."

That evening Harry treated us all to a meal in a bar at the lower end of the village which we reached through the narrow, meandering streets. Geoff pointed out a couple of For Sale signs in English, but I didn't think Harry would mind having a few British neighbours, though I hoped they wouldn't all be southerners, as he usually becomes even more deaf in their presence; yet another of his trifling prejudices which I was sure that Laura would iron out, given time.

When we waved goodbye to Laura the following morning it was au revoir rather than adiós, as Harry would be with her shortly, they would both see Geoff all too soon, and I was sure that June would be up for an autumn trip to such an appealing place.

Laura and Harry had clearly cemented their budding relationship and I don't think there was any doubt in either of their minds that they would be together and probably marry in the foreseeable future. Though they were sociable with us when we met, they did spend quite a lot of time alone, but I'm not in a position to say more about that, and I knew better than to quiz Harry about the ups and downs of their connubial endeavours.

"So we'll take the motorway to Malaga and then head inland to Ronda, shall we?" I asked from the driver's seat.

"Why not head straight down the motorway to Gib," said Geoff.

"Shut up," said Harry from the back.

"Well, it's you two who keep telling me I've got to earn some money, and now you're preventing me from doing it," he said with his clever dick smile.

"You've still got your twenty-odd grand to be going on with and you'll get a few quid for that old motorbike of yours," said Harry.

"Oh, I couldn't part with my Harley," Geoff said, looked over at me.

"Does it leak oil?"

"Of course not."

"Then it can stay in my garage, for now, but that'll leave less room for your other stuff."

"Fair enough. I'm not one of those people who accumulate baggage. Life's for living, not for hoarding."

"I've got tons of stuff. I guess I'll rent one of those storage units," said Harry, never one to put upon his friends.

"That's good. Geoff can share a bit of it with you."

"Oh, there'll be no need…"

I report that fascinating exchange merely to underline what I said earlier about the spiritual decline of our journey, as both my friends had their minds on other things, especially Geoff, who already dreamt of driving Ferraris down through Europe and making fat commissions when he sold them. Harry at least made an effort to reintroduce our old pioneering spirit, especially when he insisted that we should wild camp one more time.

"But somewhere miles from anywhere this time. We haven't even emptied Bambi's water deposit yet, that's how soft we've been."

"We haven't had to bury our shit either," I said, quite relieved about that.

"Exactly. We probably won't be doing this again, so let's get right away from it all for one night."

I glanced up at the blue sky. "Let's do it tonight then, as it's sure to stay fine."

Within an hour and a half we had passed the sprawling city of Malaga, which none of us wished to visit, though I now know that it's an interesting, attractive place. The dual-carriageway ended just after passing a town called Cártama and we could see mountains to the west, so I decided to head straight for them. According to the map, Yunquera appeared to be the last large village before the sierra that loomed behind it, and a pleasant place it turned out to be; tidied up for the tourist trade, I guessed, but still unspoilt. We bought our provisions before lunch, knowing that the shops would close until about five, and enjoyed a tasty *menu del día* at a bar on the main road.

Over coffee, as had become my habit, I opened the map.

"Right, we'll fill up with fuel and then head north along here until we find a decent forest road into the sierra. Are you both OK with that?"

"Yep."

"If we *have* to."

"Once we leave the road there'll be no more amenities, so if you want me to find a campsite on my phone, tell me now."

"There's bound to be one near Ronda," said Geoff.

"Nope, we're going to rough it. Making memories is what corny folk call it, and we're going to make a few tonight," said Harry. "Once we leave the road I don't want to see a soul until tomorrow."

"It seems a bit pointless to me," said Geoff.

"Or the day after if you don't stop whining."

A few miles to the north of Yunquera a large green sign indicated that one could enter the Sierra de las Nieves, so I turned left and trundled along the track, confident that we'd left civilisation behind for the time being. That big sign should have warned me though, as after less than a mile we reached one of those picnic areas, this one with a large white building beside it.

"This'll do," said Geoff.

"Bollocks, there's some cars and a minibus over there."

"Let's have a look anyway."

The building proved to be an old watermill which had been converted into a rural hostel, and the minibus proved to contain a group of teenagers about to enjoy a weekend in the country.

"This won't do at all," said Harry as we observed the Spanish kids, whose idea of conversation appeared to be to all talk at the same time.

"On we go then, into the wilderness," I said, making for Bambi before the youngsters saw it, to no avail, as we drove out of there to a chorus of hoots and whistles. Less than a mile later we passed another cluster of buildings, from where it appeared that one could ride horses and take part in 'multi-adventures', whatever that meant, but after that it was just us, nature, the purring of Bambi's steadfast engine and the rattling of her contents. The track continued through the woods close to a stream, but to my disappointment turned into an impassable trail, as I'd hoped to find a route right through the sierra which would bring us out not too far from Ronda.

"This is the end of the road then," I said, parking up on a flat bit beneath the pine trees. "It's a bit rough for pitching your tent, Harry."

"I think I'll use that bivvy bag of yours, if that's all right with you. I want to get really close to nature tonight. I want to feel it on my face."

"You might feel snakes on your face, or scorpions," said Geoff with a guttural giggle.

"So no airbed then?" I asked.

Harry looked at the rough ground. "Hmm, well, I might use it."

"Soft git," said Geoff.

"If it'd been up to you, we'd have been in Malaga airport by now, so shut it."

After getting out the chairs and table our little forest nook began to look quite cosy and I almost regretted that we hadn't been so intrepid before. As the sun began to near the mountain ridge it became pleasantly cool and I thought it a pity that fires weren't allowed.

"Let's have a fire," said Geoff as we drank our first beer.

"It's not permitted outside the picnic area," I said.

"Oh, they just say that so the townies don't burn the forest down. We could make a little one just there."

I looked down at the dry scrubby ground and up at the canopy of pine trees.

"No way," said Harry before I did. "This is a bloody tinder box. We'll make do with some candles."

By the time we'd eaten what proved to be our last three-can combination – curry, beans and I forget what else – night was falling, so we stuck three candles on our little table, much more atmospheric than the electric lantern. The flickering light, and maybe the beer and wine we'd drunk, seemed to bring us closer together and I hoped that Geoff wouldn't remember he had a guitar, now stored out of sight above the cab.

"This is nice," I said, not the most original conversation starter, but it worked.

"I'm glad we've come now. We should have done more of this instead of going to bourgeois campsites," said Geoff.

"I'm glad we went to the one at Las Negras. Me and Laura will go back there sometime, maybe a year after we met."

"Yes, that was a stroke of luck," I said.

"Fate, I reckon," Harry said, turning his eyes on Geoff. "That's what you should do?"

"What?"

"Nothing. Instead of sniffing after every piece of skirt you see, you should just sit back and wait for the right woman to come along."

"Well, I might just be able to do that when I'm living in my seafront apartment and driving posh cars around. Bambi hasn't helped matters, or being with you two, but all that'll change when I get back to Torre del Mar."

"Don't start spending money until you're earning it though. Weigh up your prospects with this Hugo chap and play it by ear," I said, having always been fond of giving noncommittal advice, like on Careers Day at my former school.

"I hope it works out, I really do, because it's about time you settled to something," said Harry in an almost fatherly tone. "It won't get any easier to get jobs from now on, so you'd better make the best of this one."

"Or find something else if you see it's not working out," I added.

"Whoa, boys! What's this? A counselling session? I'm quite capable of looking after myself, you know."

"We have your best interests at heart," I said, beginning to enjoy this two-pronged attack of benevolence. "The thing is that Harry and I... well, touch wood, our lives are just about sorted." I reached down to tap a twig on the ground. "We've both got good pensions and a woman we love, so it's only natural that we should want you to have the same."

"Stands to reason," said Harry, nodding sagely.

"We're older than you too, so we see things from a slightly different perspective."

"One that you'll be seeing just six short years from now," said Harry.

"And we want you to feel then like we do now." I looked at Harry.

"Empathy, you'd probably call it."

"Or brotherly love... no, avuncular love."

"What's that when it's at home?" Harry asked.

"Uncly love."

"Yes, we do worry about you, Geoff, like uncles."

"But we know you won't let us down," I said.

"Like by buying one of the cars that you're supposed to be selling."

"Or renting a penthouse."

"Or doing things for Hugo that aren't strictly legal."

"Or shacking up with a floozy," I said.

"That's enough!" Geoff cried, covering his ears. "Stop now before I begin to think you're taking the piss."

Then we all had a good laugh, which made us thirsty, so I went inside for another bottle of wine.

"You know, we could stay here for another night," Geoff said sleepily a while later.

"Or two. We've still got plenty of tins," said Harry.

"The air seems chilly, but I don't feel cold at all," I said.

"It's great here. I think I'll get in my sack, if you don't mind," said Harry, stretching his arms.

"Go ahead."

"Feel free."

A while later, Geoff and I clambered into Bambi and I was soon dead to the world. It's an indication of how soundly I slept that I didn't hear the rain rattling down on the roof until it was light. A shower, I thought, and turned over to sleep some more, before being finally awoken by Geoff's voice.

"Bloody hell!" he cried from the doorway. "There's been a monsoon. Come and look at this."

I lifted my aching head from the pillow and unzipped my bag, before tottering over to the doorway that Geoff had vacated in order to sit on his bed and double up with laughter. It was still raining, though not hard, but when I looked down I saw Harry in the bivvy bag upon the airbed, surrounded by water and fast asleep.

"He must be drenched," Geoff said with glee.

"I think those bags are waterproof. That's the whole point of them."

"Yes, but some must have got in where his big fat head is."

"I'd better wake him."

"No, take some photos first, for posterity."

I had to admit that for the sake of a few minutes, Harry's sodden state ought to be immortalised, so I switched on my smartphone and clicked away from the van.

"Give it here," said Geoff, before snatching the phone and jumping down into the puddles in his bare feet. "We need to cover every angle," he added, slowly circling Harry before finally getting a few close-ups of his dripping face.

He brought me the phone before splashing back to the body and crouching down.

"Ha-rry, Ha-rry," he murmured in his ear.

Harry opened one eye, then the other, before licking his lips. A hand then rose from within the bag and stroked his face, by which time he had an inkling that he was wet. He sat up and was about to roll off his life raft when Geoff steadied him.

"Don't do anything rash, Harry. We can save you yet," he said, clearly having the time of his life.

I decided to give a bit of moral support, so I kicked off my sandals and joined them in the swamp. By carefully pulling down the bivvy bag and then unzipping the sleeping bag, we managed to aid Harry up off the airbed in a remarkably dry state, before we all repaired to the van to assess the situation.

"Why did you leave me out there?" Harry asked.

"We didn't know," I said.

"Until twenty minutes ago. Don't worry, we've got some pictures of your ordeal."

"It was no ordeal, thanks to that," he said, pointing at the airbed, now almost afloat in the hollow where he had chosen to bed down.

By the time we'd dried our feet and put on the kettle the rain had stopped and the clouds were beginning to shift.

"The sooner we get out of here the better," Geoff said. "I knew we should have gone down the coast. We could be eating an English breakfast in Gib now."

"Some Hispanophile you are. We'd better take a look at the track before we try to drive back to the road," I said, though Bambi appeared to be on fairly solid ground.

An hour later the sun was shining and the puddles had all but disappeared. Harry deflated the airbed and hung it from a branch to dry while I washed our cups in the swollen stream. I also made use of the trowel for the first time, deep in the woods, before handing it over to Harry.

"Well, that was a wild wild camp," I said when we gathered together again.

"And we've certainly made some memories," said Geoff.

"Especially you two, though I like the photos. I'll tell folk down the pub we did stuff like this every night."

"The pub you won't be visiting for much longer," I said.

"No, but I'm sure I'll find a bar I like in Canillas. Come on, let's get back on the road."

We waited a while longer for the airbed and the canvas chairs to dry, before Geoff, being the lightest, climbed into the driver's seat and reversed cautiously onto the track.

"I reckon Bambi's probably amphibious anyway," Harry said.

"She looks peculiar enough to be. You go up front. You deserve a proper seat."

15

After driving slowly back to the road we headed north to the pretty village of El Burgo, perched on a hill with great views of the craggy ridge beyond it. After eating a belated breakfast, Geoff drove us west on a narrow, twisting road into the Serranía de Ronda.

"Great cycling country," said Geoff.

"You'll not get me on a bike again," said Harry.

"I might try it again, but not in England with all that damn traffic," I said. It was about then that a new thought began to emerge in my still fairly flexible mind, that maybe June and I could come to live in Spain too. It wasn't something that we'd considered when we came to make our retirement plans, so I thought it best to say nothing about it and see what she thought of inland Spain when we came out to see Harry and Geoff, hopefully later in the year. I can see why Spain attracts so many British people, but being a keen walker I'd be loath to exchange our cool summers near the Lakes for the excruciating heat which was only just beginning, especially inside Bambi when she crawled up the inclines. Still, I was more than pleased that Harry had met a charming woman who happened to have a large house in a pretty village set in stunning countryside, so maybe I should be content with that for the time being, I thought as the road straightened a little as we neared the top of what proved to be the *Puerto del Viento*, or Windy Pass, at 1190 metres above sea-level.

We stopped to admire the views of the rugged, rather dry mountains, before beginning the long descent towards Ronda. Much has been written about this famous white town and its tremendous gorge, so I'll leave it to abler pens than my own to describe its beauty, save to say that the *Puente Nuevo*, or New Bridge, built in the eighteen century, really is a remarkable feat of engineering. Considering that it took many months to repair a few small bridges in the Lake District affected by the recent floods, one wonders how they managed to build a bridge straddling a hundred metre chasm without machinery, though I believe it took over thirty years and many people died in the endeavour, health and safety not being quite what it is today.

Geoff complained about the number of tourists, but I told him that he'd better get used to them if he was going to live on the Malaga coast.

"Oh, I expect I'll get a place up in the hills once I've made a bit of money," he said as we sat under the shade of a café terrace watching the people go by.

"What's the plan now?" Harry asked.

"There's a campsite on the edge of town, if you want to stay there," I said.

"Hmm, we've seen the gorge and I'm not all that keen on all these folk either. This is the sort of place I might come to with Laura; you know, to stroll about and look at the shops."

"Yes, June would like it here."

"I'll probably come with a bird too, when I'm driving something especially smart," said Geoff. "So why don't we press on to the south."

I opened the map. Heading south would take us dangerously close to the coast and as soon as Geoff got a whiff of sea air he'd begin to pester us about heading down to Gibraltar. I saw that the road west entered another *Parque Natural*, so I suggested going that way.

"There's a village call Grazalema not all that far away which is supposed to be really nice, and there's a campsite nearby," I said, crossing my fingers under the table.

"How do you know?" Geoff asked, his eyebrows arched with suspicion.

"Oh, I was using the Wi-Fi while I was waiting for you in Torre del Mar and I spotted it."

This wasn't true, but I reckoned that as the natural park was named after the village it was bound to be pretty and ought to boast camping facilities.

"Yep, we'll go that way," said Harry, so the decision was made.

Fortunately Grazalema was great. We reached it after a twenty mile drive during which the scenery improved all the time. The mountains weren't especially high, but the road was lovely; often tree-lined, but occasionally the vista opened up before us and we could see rolling pastureland and craggy peaks in the distance. Our first sight of the village was all I could have hoped for, as it clung to the green hillside with a prominent triangular peak just behind it. When we parked Bambi and went for a wander it soon became clear that we were by no means the first tourists to reach it, as there seemed to be a bar or restaurant on every corner, many of them still busy at four o'clock on a Saturday.

"At least they're mostly Spanish," said Geoff.

"They certainly like eating out," Harry said with approval.

We'd had a few tapas in Ronda, so after further exploration of the less commercial streets – most of the restaurants seemed to be in one small area – we entered a quiet bar to have coffee and get out of the sun for a while. The young, monolingual waiter told

Geoff that the campsite was right on the edge of the village, so my hunch had proved to be a good one.

"That lad's got a Cádiz accent, as we're in Cádiz province now," Geoff said when he'd served us. "I told you it was different."

"Sounds the same to me. I still can't understand a word," said Harry.

"Your Spanish seems to have improved while we've been here," I said to Geoff, as I suspected that he was angling for a compliment, having been reminded of his poor initial efforts back in Cantabria.

"Yes, it's coming back slowly but surely." He looked at Harry and grinned. "Are you going to learn the language?"

"Expect so," he said, scratching his stubbly chin.

"You expect so? It won't happen overnight, you know, unless you're expecting divine intervention. Back in Jaén I remember having verb tables on the bathroom door so I could practise them while I was on the bog."

"Laura'll teach me."

"I spent a lot of time on that toilet, and I wasn't constipated. It's not easy, you know, especially when you're older."

"I think as long as he learns the basics, like how to greet people and ask for things, he'll be OK," I said. "I guess the locals just like you to make an effort."

"Shall we conjugate a few verbs now?" Geoff asked.

"I'm going to conjugate another coffee, then we'll go and find the campsite," Harry said bluntly, and even Geoff couldn't argue with that.

Being a Saturday in mid-June the campsite was quite busy and as most of the camping pitches were taken we had no choice but to install ourselves in a rather expensive four-man cabin.

"Oh well, it'll make up for last night," I said as Geoff scurried over to the best bed.

"Well, I made enough memories in the woods to last me for a while," said Harry, stretching out on his bed.

The 'restaurant quarter' was quieter that evening, so we treated ourselves to a good meal in a typically Andaluz restaurant called El Torreon. After climbing the stairs to the dining room we were led to a table by a wood-burning stove which crackled away despite the time of year, as the village is at over 800 metres and it had turned a little chilly outside. We all tried the *Sopa de Grazalema*, more of a stew than a soup, with bits of tasty sausage floating in it, and while I plumped for roast lamb for the main course, Geoff sampled the salmon and Harry got stuck into a large lump of wild boar which the waiter assured him had been roaming in the hills until very recently. Geoff insisted that the hunting season for those beasts was in winter, so maybe Harry's chunk had been poached or had lain in the freezer for a while, but he enjoyed it all the same. Harry and I washed our meals down with such a nice Rioja red that we decided to order another bottle and instructed the waiter to assemble a cheeseboard which we then scoffed in lieu of dessert for the second time on the trip. I've refrained from boring you with every meal we ate, but this one stands out in my mind and I thoroughly recommend the restaurant, the village, the campsite and the surrounding countryside, which we set out to explore the following morning.

"A swift walk and then off, eh?" Geoff said over an early breakfast in the campsite bar.

"Nope, it'll quieten down here later, so we'll stay another night," said Harry.

"And then we'll head south," Geoff said.

"We'll vote on it," said Harry.

"I suppose I'd better look into booking flights," I said. "I'm not sure how often they are from Gibraltar and it'd be nice to fly to Manchester or Liverpool if we can."

Harry glowered into his coffee. "Yes, I don't want to see London again for as long as I live. Still, don't look till tomorrow or Mr Restless here will want to be shooting off."

"Time is money," said Geoff, drumming his fingers on the table.

"Time is time, to be enjoyed," Harry countered adeptly. "Let's follow one of those walking routes that start from here. I'd like to get into double figures today, as I need to get as fit as Laura."

"Miles or kilometres?" I asked.

"Miles, and a bit quicker than I've been walking up to now."

There are many signposted walking routes from Grazalema, several of them starting from the campsite carpark, so we chose one to a village called Benaocaz, mainly because it was on my map.

"It might be a bit too far, but we can always turn round part of the way there," I said as I shouldered the pink and blue knapsack with our water and butties. We were climbing from the word go along a scenic trail that skirted up past the base of the *Peñon Grande*, that triangular peak I mentioned, and we often turned to look down on the village or up at a couple of sinister looking vultures that we spotted, but which fortunately showed little interest in us. The path proved to be one of the best we'd followed, as after the initial ascent it weaved between nearby peaks and the landscape varied between stark rock, patches of woodland and the remains of long-abandoned farms and pastures.

On reaching one derelict farmhouse we stopped for a drink and I managed to photograph a couple of mountain goats, before asking my companions if they wished to press on or head back towards the campsite. Maybe the goats inspired them, but my preference for erring on the side of caution was briskly outvoted and we began the descent towards Benaocaz. The path soon became smoother and we passed a meadow in which horned cattle stood observing our progress with what looked like approval, but I was worried that we were overstretching ourselves.

"Lads, we've been going for over two hours and I reckon we've covered at least five miles," I said. "I think we ought to turn back now as it's going to get hotter and we can't even see that village yet."

"Yes we can," said Harry, pointing at some white specks a long way down the valley, before loping away along the trail.

As Harry was the one I was most concerned about, I shrugged and followed him, as a fifteen mile walk was nothing new to me.

"No, I can't remember the last time I walked fifteen miles," Harry said when we'd entered a bar and ordered water, beer and cured ham bocadillos. The last part of the trail had been stunning and the white village was ever so quaint, but it was almost midday, we'd been walking briskly for over three hours, and Harry, though cheerful, looked tired. Over the years I've led many walks in the Lakes and the Dales and experience had taught me who was going to struggle on the homeward leg. Harry was a classic case and he began to realise it himself when he'd demolished his sandwich and polished off a beer.

"How do your legs feel now?" I asked.

"Hmm, a bit stiff," he said, stretching one out and wincing. "It's going to be a bit tough going back."

"Nah, don't be soft. You'll soon get your second wind," said Geoff.

I employed my best teacher's frown and opened the map. "I think I'm going to make an executive decision," I said as I perused the road route back. "I think we should go back on the road, so that if any of us get tired we can hopefully hitch a lift."

Geoff turned the map round. "But it's longer that way, quite a bit longer."

"Yes, it looks like the road drops down about a mile beyond the village, but it should be a nice one and there are bound to be a few cars, it being Sunday."

Geoff screwed up his nose. "Sounds like a daft idea to me."

"What do you reckon, Harry?" I asked.

"I'll nip to the loo and think about it."

When he returned he said his legs felt like lead and that, on the whole and all things considered, the road might be the best bet.

"That's settled then. All right, Geoff?"

"Hmm, it'll be a cop-out if we hitch, and I'm not tired. I know! I'll nip back along the path and if you don't turn up I'll come and get you in Bambi."

"Are you sure?" I asked, not dismayed by the idea as the road looked like a very minor one and it was conceivable that very few cars would pass and none of them might be willing to pick up a sweaty, dishevelled man-mountain like Harry, or me, for that matter.

"Yep, I reckon I can get back in a couple of hours, so I'll have a dip in the pool and then come and find you."

A while later Harry and I set off down the road and I was relieved to see a few cars coming towards us. After a mile downhill and another uphill, Harry said that if a car came our way he wouldn't be averse to hopping into it.

"I think I'll have done my ten miles soon and I'm a bit knackered. How far is it now?"

"Another ten miles, I think."

He looked over his shoulder, before adjusting his cap and plodding on.

The trouble was that all the cars were heading towards Benaocaz, presumably to have lunch in one of the restaurants there, and so far none had come in our direction. We were walking up a long drag at that point and the scenery was lovely, but Harry was no longer looking at it, preferring to inspect the tarmac a couple of yards in front of him, sweat dripping from his nose. By the time we reached the small village of Villaluenga del Rosario he appeared to be on his last legs, but put on a slight spurt when he saw a roadside bar, where he drank a can of coke and slumped back in his chair.

"Sorry about this, Jeremy."

"It happens. I think I'd struggle to walk back in this heat too. Let's see if the waiter speaks English."

He did, of sorts, and we were delighted to hear that a bus went from Benaocaz to Grazalema and stopped just up the road.

"Muy bien. A qué hora?" I asked.

"About four o'clock. Better you stand in road so he stop," said the pleasant youth. "You like eat?"

"Yes, please."

Given that we had two hours to kill, we had a leisurely, abundant lunch and made great efforts to rehydrate ourselves, first with water, then beer, and plenty of it.

"Guess we should be outside in case Geoff comes past," Harry said at about three, content but drowsy.

"Too hot out there. Besides, he's probably still walking, then he'll collapse in a heap when he gets back." I yawned. "No chance of us missing him."

We both dozed on the short bus journey back and after trudging up to the campsite we were shocked to see a patch of bare grass where Bambi had been.

"She's either been pinched or Geoff's gone to find us," I said, beginning to giggle.

"He must have passed us."

"Oh dear, and he'll be ever so tired. Shame he didn't bring a phone."

"Shall we stay in the cabin or go for a dip?"

"A swim might sober us up. We'll leave a note," I said, before we both creased up with laughter.

"You rotten lousy bastards," were Geoff's first words when the sunburnt shadow of his former self appeared at the pool within which we were recuperating after our ordeal.

"We were on the bus. Did you not see us?" I said, looking suitably repentant.

"Obviously not. I drove right back to that blasted village and spent half an hour asking after you. Then I stopped where you had your, and I quote, 'very big food and much beers,' and found out that you'd caught the bloody bus."

"How was the walk back?" Harry asked, his mouth unnaturally rigid.

"Hot. Hot and knackering. It took me ages, but I got straight in the van and came to get you, thinking you'd be suffering in the heat."

I began to wade towards the steps. "I'll go and get your towel and trunks."

"I can get them myself," he snapped, before stomping off, limping slightly.

"He's annoyed," said Harry.

"Yes, just imagine walking all that way and then that happening."

"A bummer. Still, that's what friends are for."

"He'll see that, given time," I said. "How can we ever repay him?"

"By getting down to Gib within a couple of days, I guess."

"Hmm, it's not that far off now. We could have one more night on the way and then call it a day," I said.

"That'd suit me. Whatever we do now, we won't beat today for..."

"Pure entertainment?"

"That's it, though I hope he's not pissed off for the rest of the day."

I nodded, thought, and nodded again. "He won't be, you'll see."

By telling Geoff that in view of his great selflessness in the face of adversity we had decided to sacrifice our own desire to prolong the trip and instead reach Gibraltar within two days, he was soon mollified.

"We could drive straight there tomorrow," he said after a good soak in the pool.

"Nope, one more night, somewhere nice," said Harry.

"How about on The Rock?" said Geoff.

"There's a flight to Manchester at about eight in the evening on Tuesday, the day after tomorrow," I said, as I'd been doing my homework. "I don't want to spend our last night on British territory, so I agree with Harry. We stay somewhere good tomorrow night, then drive down on Tuesday."

Geoff nodded and splashed about a bit, before his eyes popped open. "Hey, what about Bambi?"

"She's your van," said Harry.

"We could arrive a bit earlier and you could see if some garage will give you anything for her," I said, having also forgotten about our vehicle's future since Geoff's European tour had been scrapped in favour of working for the Belgian Del Boy.

"I'll have a think," Geoff said, before his head disappeared beneath the water.

While Harry and Geoff enjoyed early evening naps, I booked the flights for Tuesday and was able to print out the boarding passes in the campsite reception. As we would soon be eating our penultimate dinner together on Spanish soil, for the time being, I did a little research and later led them to a 'Gastrobar' on one of the cobbled streets some way from the main restaurant quarter. After admiring the bull's head lovingly mounted on the wall, and a series of bull-related photos, mainly of folk dragging one around on a long rope, we sat on the terrace and enjoyed the cool evening air.

Two young ladies who appeared to be sisters ran the bar and the tapas really were quite exquisite. A hungry Geoff attacked every plate with relish, while Harry and I, still partly sated after our big lunch, sampled each dish in a more dignified manner. I especially enjoyed the partridge croquettes and the Iberian pork cheeks, but it was all delicious and didn't set me back too much.

"Thanks for that, Jeremy," Harry said as he sipped his brandy. "I'll treat you both tomorrow night."

"What about me? I'm not a pauper, you know," said a glowing Geoff.

"No, and you'll soon be loaded when you've flogged Bambi," Harry laughed.

"Ah," said Geoff, before looking up at the starlit sky in a meaningful way.

Harry and I looked at each other and I unfolded the map, which we began to study earnestly.

"Aren't you going to ask me what I'm going to do with the van?" Geoff asked.

"Nope," said Harry.

"Surprise us," I said.

"I will then, but you'll never guess."

"It wouldn't be a surprise if we did," I said before tracing a possible route towards the coast, causing Harry to nod with approval, while Geoff just sighed and fidgeted.

"I'll give you three guesses," he finally said.

"What about?" Harry asked.

"Bambi, of course. Three guesses, go on."

"You're going to donate her to the Barbary apes as a winter retreat," I said.

"Humph."

"You're going to turn her into an ice-cream van and ply your wares along the coast?" said Harry.

"I've already got a job, and a good one."

"One guess left, Harry," I said.

"Best not waste it."

"No, I'll let you take a shot."

"No, you've got a logical mind, Jeremy. I'll leave it to you."

"Let's toss for it."

I tossed a Euro and won.

"You're going to… you're going to… no, it won't come. No, wait… you're going to…" I grimaced and kneaded my temples. "You're going to… raffle her at the airport."

"Ha ha," he said with irony and loathing. "Now you'll just have to wait and see."

"You got any sleeping pills, Jeremy?" Harry asked me.

"Yes, we'd better take some or we won't get a wink tonight," I said.

"Or tomorrow night, as there's no way I'm telling you now."

"Fair enough," said Harry, bending his stiff legs before pushing himself to his feet. "Last campsite snooze tonight."

"Is it?" I asked.

"I reckon so. I think we deserve a hotel for our last night, then we don't have to mess about packing stuff up on Tuesday."

"Hardly an adventurous end to our trip, is it?" said Geoff, still smarting after our pitiful lack of curiosity regarding Bambi's fate.

"No, but I like the idea," I said. "Let's vote on it. Who says hotel?"

Two hands shot up, before Geoff swatted the air and called us wimps. "Still, it's not the last chance I'll get to... no, I'm not telling you."

When he later went to clean his teeth Harry and I hazarded genuine guesses as to Bambi's likely future. Our conjectures coincided and we both turned out to be right.

16

I won't keep you for much longer, as there's no surprise ending or unexpected bombshell coming up, because I've tried to adhere pretty much to the truth in the writing of this account. The following morning we struck camp at ten and set off towards the town of Ubrique.

"This road looks familiar," said Harry after a couple of miles in the passenger seat.

"Not to me, not this bit anyway, as I think I was fast asleep at the time," I replied from the back.

"Don't remind me," said our driver.

Apart from pointing out where we'd eaten and drunk our fill, we didn't torment Geoff too much about the previous day's debacle, even when we drove past Benaocaz, after which we began to climb a short but snaky pass from the top of which we caught a fleeting glimpse of Ubrique. A mile or two later we saw the white town stretched along the rocky mountainside and were all keen to take a closer look. After trundling through the newer streets we saw the old town up ahead, so Geoff parked near a bank and we strolled off to explore.

We all agreed that it was a lovely town, but likewise concurred that we had that 'journey's end' feeling and wished to do little more than take it easy and soak up the atmosphere of a town that might well form part of a future itinerary for Harry and Laura, June and I, or Geoff and the flash bird he would soon meet.

"We could all come together on a tour of the white towns," Geoff said as we sipped a beer in the shade of a terrace, just for a change.

"You've got to meet the lucky lady yet," I said.

"Give me a month… or two. Once I get some decent wheels and a nice pad the world'll be my oyster again."

"When was the world last your oyster?" Harry asked.

"Oh, on and off all my life. I'm not set in my ways like you two."

"You can hardly call Harry set in his ways," I protested. "He's about to start a new life with a new woman in a new country."

"True. You're a lucky man, Harry."

"Thanks."

"Having me so close by. I reckon I can whizz up that road in half an hour in a decent motor, tractors permitting."

"And Bambis," I said.

"Ha ha, and Bambis, yes," he said, raising his eyebrows in an exaggerated fashion.

"Shall we find a hotel here?" Harry asked quickly.

"Could do, or maybe press on a bit," I said. "It's still quite a way to the coast."

"OK, but the first smart-looking hotel we see, we stay there," Harry said. "Otherwise we'll get too near and we'll feel like we're just waiting to leave."

In the end we wandered around a bit more, before lunching on another restaurant terrace and setting off southwards. We'd covered barely a mile when Harry slapped the dashboard and said, "Stop, we'll stay there."

"It looks posh," I said, glancing over at the imposing white and red hotel on the outskirts of town. With its two storeys of arched windows it looked a bit like a stately home, but was clearly quite new.

"I don't care. I'll pay and you two can get dinner," said Harry. "A bit of luxury never killed anyone and it'll round off the trip nicely."

After checking into our individual rooms on the second floor with great views to the west, we all had a siesta, before rendezvousing in the hotel bar at six. The only downside to the place was that it was a long way from the town centre, and as I thought it wise to take June a gift of some sort, we jumped in the van and headed back in. Ubrique is famous for its leather, so after ambling around a few of the numerous shops, I bought her a stylish beige handbag, while Harry got Laura a darker one, and Geoff selected an ornate and even more expensive bag for his hypothetical lover. Back at the hotel, which is festooned with dead animal heads, it being a popular haunt of hunters, we sampled the *carne de caza*, or game meat, at dinner, before chilling out on the lovely patio for a while.

"I can't help thinking that we should be in Bambi for our last night," said Geoff, instead of being grateful that Harry had coughed up for the hotel, which he later told me wasn't as dear as it looked.

"Well, we've had plenty of use out of her and she's been damned reliable," I said.

"I'm keeping my airbed as a keepsake of the trip," said Harry.

"Your bag'll be lighter, without all those tins," I said.

"They won't go to waste," said Geoff, gazing enigmatically across the almost deserted terrace, as few animals can be shot in June.

"Yes, I'm sure someone'll enjoy them," I said.

"Some poor sap, I expect," Harry said.

"I'm off to bed," said Geoff, maybe guessing that we had an inkling as to the fate of our trusty steed.

The following day we arrived at La Linea de la Concepción at about one. We'd passed through the lovely white villages of Cortes de la Frontera and Gaucín – from where we got our first distant view of The Rock and the coast of Africa beyond – before the road gradually straightened and widened, prior to the last few miles down the motorway. The sprawling town has benefited from Gibraltar's proximity and unique status – many locals work there and smuggling has always been a nice little earner – but seemed to have little to recommend it and justify Geoff's seemingly aimless meandering around the outlying streets.

"What on earth are we doing, Geoff?" I asked, though I had a pretty good idea.

"You'll see," he replied, smiling inscrutably.

After touring round a few more blocks of nondescript flats he pulled into a diagonal parking space, yanked on the handbrake, turned off the ignition, and slapped the steering wheel.

"The end of the road, for now," he said, turning to face Harry, before leering at me in the back.

"Are we supposed to walk from here?" Harry asked.

"Afraid so. It's only a mile or so. Bambi's staying here for the time being."

"Ah," said Harry.

"Right," said I, before pushing myself up from the mid-corridor camping chair for the last time. "Let's get going then."

"Aren't you going to ask me what's going to happen to her?" Geoff whined.

"I guess you're just dumping her," I said.

"A sad fate, but probably for the best," said Harry, patting the dashboard. "Goodbye, faithful friend."

"Well I'm not. A week from now I'll be back and I'll drive her up to Torre del Mar."

"You don't' say?" I cried.

"Well I never!" said Harry.

"Your ingenuity astonishes me, Geoff."

"I'd never have twigged in a million months of Sundays."

"So you both guessed then?"

"Yep."

"Just about. We thought you might find a better place to leave her than here, but we knew you were going to keep her."

Then later as we sipped a final beer overlooking Gibraltar's marina.

"Good idea to hang onto Bambi though," I said to dispel the remains of Geoff's slight sulkiness. "You wouldn't have got much for her and she's been worth her weight in gold really. I'm glad you're keeping her."

"Not exactly a flash set of wheels to impress the birds with though," said Harry. "You might pick up a hippy, but not a decent girl."

"Ha, very good. I'm hoping that Hugo'll let me store her at his place until I decide what to do with her. She's still got seven months' MOT, so there's time, or maybe I'll register her here, who knows."

"Here's to Bambi, the van that carried three old chaps right across Spain," I said, raising my glass.

"Two," Geoff murmured.

We clinked glasses and drank to the van, our trip and the future.

THE END

22104751R00134

Printed in Poland
by Amazon Fulfillment
Poland Sp. z o.o., Wrocław